Samuel Richardson

THE PROFILES IN LITERATURE SERIES

GENERAL EDITOR : B. C. SOUTHAM, M.A., B LITT. (OXON.)
*Formerly Department of English, Westfield College,
University of London*

Volumes in the series include

CHARLOTTE BRONTË	Arthur Pollard, *University of Hull*
CHARLES DICKENS	Martin Fido, *University of Leeds*
HENRY FIELDING	C. J. Rawson, *University of Warwick*
JAMES JOYCE	Arnold Goldman, *University of Sussex*
HERMAN MELVILLE	D. E. S. Maxwell, *Professor of English, York Univ. Toronto*
THOMAS LOVE PEACOCK	Carl Dawson, *University of California*
WALTER SCOTT	Robin Mayhead, *University of Ghana*
JONATHAN SWIFT	Kathleen Williams, *University of California*
ZOLA	Philip Walker, *University of California*

Samuel Richardson

by A. M. Kearney
Lecturer in English
Chorley College of Education

LONDON

ROUTLEDGE & KEGAN PAUL

NEW YORK: HUMANITIES PRESS

First published 1968
by Routledge and Kegan Paul Ltd
Broadway House, 68–74 Carter Lane
London, E.C.4

Printed in Great Britain
by Northumberland Press Limited
Gateshead

SBN 7100 2945 4

The Profiles in Literature Series

This series is designed to provide the student of literature and the general reader with a brief and helpful introduction to the major novelists and prose writers in English, American and foreign literature.

Each volume will provide an account of an individual author's writing career and works, through a series of carefully chosen extracts illustrating the major aspects of the author's art. These extracts are accompanied by commentary and analysis, drawing attention to particular features of the style and treatment. There is no pretence, of course, that a study of extracts can give a sense of the works as a whole, but this selective approach enables the reader to focus his attention upon specific features, and to be informed in his approach by experienced critics and scholars who are contributing to the series.

The volumes will provide a particularly helpful and practical form of introduction to writers whose works are extensive or which present special problems for the modern reader, who can then proceed with a sense of his bearings and an informed eye for the writer's art.

An important feature of these books is the extensive reference list of the author's works and the descriptive list of the most useful biographies, commentaries and critical studies.

B.C.S.

Contents

CONTENTS

CONTENTS

Samuel Richardson—his life and works

Life and early writings

Samuel Richardson (1689–1761) is one of the most interesting figures in English Literature. By the age of fifty or so, he had produced nothing more remarkable in the literary way than a few indexes and prefaces, and these were merely the outcome of his business as a printer. Yet less than ten years later, he was an established figure of the literary scene, numbering celebrities like Johnson and Garrick among his acquaintances.

There was certainly little enough in Richardson's early life to suggest his future as a successful novelist. The main facts are set out with characteristic complacency in a lengthy autobiographical sketch which he sent to an interested Dutch correspondent in 1753. At an early age, he was apprenticed to a printer and by a process of industrious self-improvement and shrewd manoeuvre (he married his master's daughter) rose to a considerable position in the trade. He was, it appears, a model apprentice, taking time out of his rest periods to improve his mind by reading, and taking care that even the candle should be of his own purchasing. After such a beginning, we are hardly surprised to learn that once he had set up business on his own, he pursued his work 'with an Assiduity that, perhaps, has few Examples'.

It was this assiduity, however, which brought him into contact with the bookselling world, and no one was readier than Richardson to oblige the booksellers with 'abstracting, abridging, compiling, and giving (an) Opinion of Pieces offered them'. He was, moreover, skilled in epistolary matters, having begun at an early age, so he claims, by writing an expostulatory letter to a hypocritical widow of fifty with such address that he was only discovered by his handwriting; and throughout his apprenticeship, had kept up a correspondence with a gentleman who was a 'Master of ye Epistolary Style'.

Whatever the truth about all this, there can be no doubt that Richardson's talents as a model writer were well known to the publishing world of the time. It is not really surprising then that he should have been asked in 1739 by two booksellers to prepare a volume of model letters dealing with situations requiring practical advice, and designed to help 'country readers' unskilled in penmanship. This wholesome collection was precisely to Richardson's taste, but the important thing is that it made demands upon his imaginative powers as well as his advisory ones. The situations he chose to illustrate were various, but one of them (the situation of handsome girls in service who might be subject to plots against their virtue) put him in mind of a story he had heard some years previously, concerning a particular servant-girl and her designing master. This story was the germ of *Pamela*, and setting the model letters aside, Richardson embarked upon his career as a novelist.

The three novels which followed, *Pamela* (1740), *Clarissa*

(1748), and *Sir Charles Grandison* (1754) were all produced to the same moral plan. Richardson's avowed intent was to 'promote the cause of religion and virtue' and to this extent, the novels may be regarded as a logical continuation of the model letters. But there was much more to them than this. The novel form allowed Richardson's creative talents much greater freedom than the model letters had, and despite his public sermonising, by the end of his first novel, Richardson had moved a long way beyond his simple intentions. The epistolary technique proved to be a brilliantly successful means of bringing the reader to a new kind of involvement, and this technique was enhanced by the daring nature of his themes. In short, Richardson had made fiction at once more sensational than formerly, and at the same time (as he insisted) more instructive. In having the best of both worlds, it is not surprising that the reading public (at this time rapidly expanding) raved over his novels.

Pamela

While a demonstration of Richardson's real powers must wait till later, it may be useful at this point to have a very brief summary of the three stories which caused such a stir in the literary circles of the day. *Pamela* concerns the fortunes of a clever and virtuous servant-girl, Pamela Andrews, who on the death of her kind mistress finds herself pursued by the young son, Mr. B., who is now her master. The more Pamela resists his advances, the keener Mr. B. becomes, and the more desperate his stratagems to trap her. Finally, he agrees to send her home to her parents, but by a trick has her taken off to Lincolnshire instead, installing her in a lonely house with two frightful warders,

Mrs. Jewkes and Colbrand, to watch over her. Pamela unsuccessfully tries to escape, and even contemplates suicide. Meanwhile, Mr. B. arrives and continues his attempts at seduction with no more success than before. He offers her generous terms to become his mistress and even suggests marriage (though all he has in mind at this stage is a mock-marriage). At last, convinced that Pamela is proof against all temptation, he offers to let her go home. But by this time it is quite apparent that neither can really do without the other, and before Pamela has gone very far, on receiving a distracted appeal from Mr. B., she decides to return to him. Her virtue is finally rewarded when he offers a genuine marriage proposal, which she accepts with gratitude. Part II is much less exciting and is simply a commentary on their married life together.

Clarissa

Clarissa has a much more complex plot than *Pamela*, but follows the career of a heroine no less talented and beautiful than Pamela. Clarissa's accomplishments like Pamela's prove a mixed blessing : on the one hand they excite admiration and delight, on the other, a fury of jealousy and intrigue. Clarissa's family are anxious that she should marry profitably and have in mind a rich, but thoroughly objectionable character called Solmes. In her anxiety to avoid this fate, Clarissa reluctantly turns for advice to a plausible young rake named Lovelace, who promises to help her. As Clarissa's family increase their pressures on her, so Lovelace increases his offers of help, designing all the while to get her away from her family. He finally succeeds in arranging a meeting with her outside the gate of her family home, Harlowe Place, and by a trick frightens

4

her into his coach and gallops off with her. Clarissa's plight is now even worse, her family refuse to have anything to do with her, and Lovelace begins to show his true colours. Having set her in a sinister house in London kept by an old bawd called Mrs. Sinclair, Lovelace makes numerous attempts to seduce her. Finding that she resists all his approaches, he then takes desperate measures and having first drugged her, rapes her. After this, Clarissa keeps in saintlike isolation, her eyes steadily on death—worldly compromise is out of the question for her. She finally returns to her family in her coffin, and the novel closes in a chorus of adulation for her unviolated principles, while Lovelace is killed in a duel by her cousin, Colonel Morden.

Sir Charles Grandison

In his final novel, *Sir Charles Grandison*, Richardson again considers the situation of an attractive heroine set loose in a world of unscrupulous males. Harriet Byron, a Northamptonshire heiress, is visiting some relations in London, when she attracts the fatal attentions of a wealthy fop, Sir Hargrave Pollexfen. Sir Hargrave, having approached her honestly and been repulsed, manages to abduct her in the Lovelace manner. He is foiled from taking any desperate measures, however, by the timely appearance of the hero Sir Charles Grandison. Sir Charles offers Harriet his protection and she is admitted to the Grandison family circle. At this juncture, there is a change of emphasis in the plot and the main centre of interest becomes Sir Charles himself. In a lengthy history of the Grandison family, Harriet hears from his sisters how Sir Charles has time and again proved his heroic qualities. Harriet's gratitude towards Sir Charles is soon turned into love. At this point, however, Sir Charles is suddenly called abroad to Italy. It seems that some time earlier he has become involved with a noble Italian family, the Porrettas, and been attracted to their daughter Clementina; marriage in fact has only been prevented on religious grounds. The remainder of the novel explores the endless ramifications of the Clementina—Sir Charles—Harriet Byron complex: will Sir Charles marry Clementina, despite the religious obstacle, or will he somehow solve the problem to the satisfaction of the Italians and return home to marry an increasingly anxious Harriet? As one might have guessed, the Italian match falls through, and Sir Charles, having acted in exemplary fashion throughout returns to England to marry Harriet. There is a slight flutter when Clementina comes to England to avoid a plan to marry her to the Count Belvedere. But all ends happily, with Sir Charles and Harriet blissfully married, and Clementina returning home with her parents much more receptive to the idea of accepting the patient Belvedere. Sir Hargrave, who has appeared on and off throughout as a minor nuisance, dies repentantly in a pathetic death-bed scene with Sir Charles by his side.

Reputation

These skeleton outlines suggest perhaps only the melodramatic element in the novels, and the new reader may well be surprised at the praise lavished on them by Richardson's contemporaries. Denis Diderot, for example, claimed that they were immortal and deserved to be placed with the works of Moses, Homer, Euripides and Sophocles, while an early admirer of *Pamela*, Knightly Chetwoode, declared that if all the books in England were to be burnt, this novel 'next the bible' ought to be saved. Certainly some readers were more critical, and indicated sanctimonious and ambiguous elements in Richardson's work (Fielding's parody *Shamela* is a delightful reminder of such criticism), but there is no denying that during the latter part of his own lifetime, and for thirty years or so after his death, no other English writer had anything like his international prestige and influence. Translations were made of the novels into all the major European languages, and countless abridgments, adaptations, and frank imitations flourished everywhere till the end of the century. (A full study of Richardson's reputation and influence has been made by A. D. McKillop in *Samuel Richardson, Printer & Novelist.* See bibliography.)

Like all cults, the Richardson cult soon extinguished itself, and for much of the following century he was rather praised than read. In recent times, however, there has been a revival of interest in him, and, detached alike from the cult and its reaction, much has been done by contemporary critics to clarify the nature of Richardson's art. There is much, of course, which is tedious and dated in his novels; there are the uncompromising moral attitudes and weak sentimentalisms which can be found at large in the literature of the period; but there is also the psychological insight and deep sense of the implications in a given emotional or moral situation. Above all, there is the undeniable control over the form in which he worked. It is now being recognised in fact, that while Richardson may have entered on a literary career by accident, and as a moralist rather than as a conscious artist, full justice yet remains to be done to his talents.

Scheme of extracts

In the following pages, we shall be considering five aspects of Richardson's art. We begin by looking at the kind of *situation* which recurs throughout the novels, and which more than anything else reveals Richardson's chief concerns. We then move on to consider his manner of *character-portrayal*—that is, of the central characters involved in these situations. Then we shall examine the way he uses surroundings to create a meaningful *atmosphere and setting* for his actions In all these areas, the fundamental importance of the *epistolary technique* will be stressed, but in the next section we shall consider some of its additional values. And finally, in looking at the kind of writing which illustrates Richardson at his most characteristically versatile, we should be in a position to make some tentative reflections about his *range and achievement*.

Much of course must be left out; for example, any thorough examination of his use of symbolism, of his linguistic originality, or of his skilful narrative control, and so on. It is hoped, however, that the features chosen will provide some indication of Richardson's abilities, and that the bibliography will suggest fruitful sources of further enquiry.

References to *Pamela* and *Clarissa* are to the Everyman's Library editions, Dent and Dutton, London and New York, 1962, and in the case of *Sir Charles Grandison*, to *The Works of Samuel Richardson*, 12 vols., Henry Sotheran & Co., London, 1883. In each case, the volume and letter number are cited, with the exception of Pamela's extensive Journal where the page number is given.

References to Richardson's own letters are to *Selected Letters of Samuel Richardson*, ed. John Carroll, OUP, London and New York, 1964, hereafter cited as *Letters*.

Basic situation

The typically recurrent situation in Richardson is one where the individual finds conflicting demands made upon his or her (usually her) integrity. In both *Pamela* and *Clarissa*, for example, the heroines are faced with a difficult choice: either to compromise their own personal sense of what is right, or to offend those (masters or parents) who make unlawful demands upon them. In the following extracts, we shall see how Richardson deals with this state of harassed integrity.

In *Pamela*, the dutiful servant-girl is faced with the unscrupulous master determined to seduce her, and here first of all, we can see her trying to reduce the problem to rational argument. Mr. B. has come upon her in the summer-house, and put his arm around her.

I

I struggled and trembled, and was so benumbed with terror, that I sunk down, not in a fit, and yet not myself; and I found myself in his arms, quite void of strength, and he

10

kissing me two or three times with frightful eagerness. At last I burst from him, and was getting out of the summer-house, but he held me back, and shut the door.

I would have given my life for a farthing. And he said, 'I'll do you no harm, Pamela; don't be afraid of me.' I said, 'I won't stay.'—'You won't, hussey!' said he: 'do you know whom you speak to?' I lost all fear and all respect, and said, 'Yes, I do, Sir, too well! Well may I forget that I am your servant, when you forget what belongs to a master.'

I sobbed and cried most sadly—'What a foolish hussey you are!' said he; 'have I done you any harm?'—'Yes, Sir,' said I, 'the greatest harm in the world: you have taught me to forget myself, and what belongs to me, and have lessened the distance that fortune had made between us, by demeaning yourself, to be so free to a poor servant. Yet, Sir, I will be bold to say, I am honest, though poor: and if you was a prince I would not be otherwise.'

He was angry, and said, 'Who would have you otherwise, you foolish slut! Cease your crying. I own I have demeaned myself! but it was only to try you: if you can keep this matter secret, you'll give me a better opinion of your prudence, and here's something,' said he, putting some gold in my hand, 'to make you amends for the fright I put you in. Go, take a walk in the garden, and don't go in till your crying is over; and I charge you to say nothing of what is past, and all shall be well, and I'll forgive you.'

'I won't take the money, indeed, Sir,' said I, 'poor as I am, I won't take it.' For, to say the truth, I thought it looked like taking earnest, and so I put it upon the bench, and as he seemed vexed and confused at what he had done, I took the opportunity to open the door, and went out of the summer-house.

He called to me, and said, 'Be secret, I charge you, Pamela, and don't go in yet, as I told you.'

O how poor and mean must those actions be, and how

little must they make the best of gentlemen look, when they offer such things as are unworthy of themselves, and put it into the power of their inferiors to be greater than they!

I took a turn or two in the garden, but in sight of the house, for fear of the worst; and breathed upon my hand to dry my eyes, because I would not be disobedient. My next (letter) shall tell you more.

Pamela, I, xi

Pamela has little difficulty here in making her point. If Mr. B. demeans himself, then she must stand up to him whatever the consequences. Personal integrity, we are in no doubt, is much more important than mere status or rank; a point further emphasised by the ironical spectacle of the master taking instruction from his servant. But while the argument about social relationship which Pamela introduces, is undoubtedly an important one (and one debated at large not only in this novel, but throughout Richardson's fiction), the situation is complicated by psychological factors. Pamela's asides—'I would have given my life for a farthing' (note the everyday colloquial touch; the comforting cliché), and her prudent, 'I thought it looked like taking earnest' (i.e., giving encouragement)— are the reactions of any young girl similarly situated; while Mr. B's blustering, 'hussey' and 'foolish slut' are determined as much by the frustrated male in him, as by the affronted master. Behind the social role, we glimpse a human figure, and beneath the social argument, a human aggressiveness. While Pamela has won the argument for the moment, therefore, the tension can by no means be dispersed with the drying of her eyes.

Marriage to Mr. B. by no means spells the end of Pamela's trials; in fact, she now finds herself as an ex-servant in a series of confrontations with her former superiors, trying to prove her right to social elevation. Once again in this next extract, we can see the familiar situation of the heroine 'on trial' defending her honour, though in a different sense than formerly. Notice as before, how both what Pamela says and the way she says it, in themselves guarantee her right to acceptance by the assembled company.

2

It was begun by Sir Jacob, who said, 'I am in love with my new niece, that I am : but still one thing sticks with me in this affair, which is, what will become of degree or distinction, if this practice of gentlemen marrying their mother's waiting-maids—excuse me, Madam—should come into vogue? Already, young ladies and young gentlemen are too apt to be drawn away thus, and disgrace their families. We have too many instances of this. You'll forgive me, both of you.'

'That,' said Lady Davers, 'is the *only* thing!—Sir Jacob has hit upon the point that would make one wish this example had not been set by a gentleman of such an ancient family, till one becomes acquainted with this dear creature, and then every body thinks it should not be otherwise than it is.'

'Ay, Pamela,' said Mr. B., 'what can you say to this? Cannot you defend me from this charge? This is a point that has been often objected to me; try for one of your pretty arguments in my behalf.'

'Indeed, Sir,' replied I, looking down, 'it becomes not me to say any thing to this.'—'But indeed it does, if you can : and I beg you'll help me to some excuse, if you have any at hand.'—'Won't you, Sir, dispense with me on this occasion? I know not what to say. Indeed I should not, if I may judge for myself, speak one *word* to this subject, for it is my absolute opinion, that degrees in general should be kept up; although I must always deem the present case an happy exception to the rule.' Mr. B. looked as if he still expected I should say something.—'Won't you, Sir, dispense with me?' repeated I. 'Indeed I should not speak to this point, if I may be my own judge.'

'I always intend, my dear, you shall judge for yourself; and, you know, I seldom urge you farther, when you use those words. But if you have any thing upon your mind to say, let's have it; for your arguments are always new and unborrowed.'

'I would then, if I *must*, Sir, ask, if there be not a nation, or if there has not been a law in some nation, which, whenever a young gentleman, be *his* degree what it would, has seduced a poor creature, be *her* degree what it would, obliges him to marry that unhappy person?'—'I think there is such a law in some country, I can't tell where,' said Sir Jacob.

'And do you think, Sir, whether it be so or not, that it is equitable it should be so?'

'Yes, by my troth. Though I must needs own, if it were so in England, many men, that I know, would not have the wives they now have.'—'You speak to your knowledge, I doubt not, Sir Jacob?' said Mr. B.

'Why, truly—I don't know but I do.'

'All then,' said I, 'that I would infer, is, whether another law would not be a still more just and equitable one, that the gentleman who is repulsed, from a principle of virtue and honour, should not be censured for marrying a person he could *not* seduce? And whether it is not more for both their honours, if he does: since it is nobler to reward a virtue, than to repair a shame, were that shame to be repaired by matrimony, which I take the liberty to doubt. But I beg your pardon: you commanded me, Sir, else this subject should not have found a speaker to it in me.'

Pamela, II, xxxiii

As before, there is a quite deliberate staging about all this. Once more the pressure is on Pamela to demonstrate and articulate her virtue before a slightly sceptical audience. Clearly she still knows her place—'it becomes not me to say any thing to this'—but when she does speak, she does so in the name of every harassed servant-girl in the kingdom and her argument is ruthlessly just. Her relationship with her audience is revealed in her modest reasonableness and the reiterative 'Sir' (cf. the previous extract), but at the same time she is also showing them up—see for example, Sir Jacob's gruff approval, 'Yes, by my troth'. As earlier, Pamela highlights the shortcomings of those who confront her : there is no such 'just and equitable' law as she suggests, but by her own qualities Pamela deserves to be on equal terms with those whose sole claim to respect is a family title. At the same time, however, her very bashfulness before her husband together with his somewhat peremptory tone—'But indeed it does, if you can' etc.— has something of the flavour of the earlier master-servant relationship. Pamela's position even in marriage is still very much a subordinate one, and Richardson throughout the novel is anxious to keep his heroine on trial. Once he has his heroines in the spotlight, he characteristically keeps them under powerful scrutiny.

While the area of confrontation has changed for Pamela B. from the backstairs to the drawing-room, marriage brings its own problems and encounters. In suggesting that her marriage is the reward for her virtuous conduct, Richardson is realistic enough to indicate the darker side of high-life. In *Clarissa*, he moves on to consider some of the complications of well-to-do family life and re-examines the marriage problem. Clarissa's family insist that she marry against her wishes thereby forcing her into a tragic

dilemma: by doing what she considers right in one sense
—i.e. refusing the unpleasant Solmes—she is bound to dis-
obey her parents, something which, as a dutiful daughter
genuinely horrifies her.

We shall now see how Richardson portrays this moral
conflict in a series of encounters between Clarissa and her
authoritarian family, bearing in mind the kind of pressur-
ised situation we have been considering in *Pamela*. Here,
first of all, Clarissa confronts her mother; notice again the
modesty of the heroine's argument and note how her
abbreviated remarks project the absolute authority of the
parent.

3

But, why, dearest madam, why am I, the *youngest*, to be
precipitated into a (marriage) state, that I am very far from
wishing to enter with anybody?

You are going to question me, I suppose, why your sister
is not thought of for Mr. Solmes?

I hope, madam, it will not displease you if I were?

I might refer you for an answer to your *father*.—Mr.
Solmes has reasons for preferring *you*—

And I have reasons, madam, for disliking *him*. And why
am I—

This quickness upon me, interrupted my mother, is not
to be borne! I am gone, and your father comes, if *I* can do
no good with you.

O madam, I would rather die, than—

She put her hand to my mouth.—No peremptoriness,
Clary Harlowe: once you declare yourself inflexible, I have
done.

I wept for vexation. This is all, all, my brother's doings
—his grasping views—

16

No reflections upon your brother; he has entirely the honour of the family at heart.

I would no more dishonour my family, madam, than my brother would.

I believe it: but I hope you will allow your father and me and your uncles to judge what will do it honour, what dishonour.

I then offered to live single; never to marry at all; or never but with their full approbation.

If you mean to show your duty and your obedience, Clary, you must show it in *our* way; not in *your own*.

I hope, madam, that I have not so behaved hitherto, as to render such a trial of my obedience necessary.

Yes, Clary, I cannot but say that you have hitherto behaved extremely well: but you have had no trials till now: and I hope, that now you are called to one you will not fail in it. Parents, proceeded she, when children are young, are pleased with every thing they do. You have been a good child upon the whole; but we have hitherto rather complied with you than you with us. Now that you are grown up to marriageable years is the test; especially as your grandfather has made you independent, as we may say, in preference to those who had prior expectations upon that estate.

Madam, my grandfather knew, and expressly mentions in his will, his desire that my father will more than make it up to my sister. I did nothing but what I thought my duty to procure his favour. It was rather a mark of his affection, than any advantage to me. For, do I either seek or wish to be independent? Were I to be Queen of the universe, that dignity should not absolve me from my duty to you and to my father. I would kneel for your blessings were it in the presence of millions—so that—

I am loth to interrupt *you*, Clary; though you could more than once break in upon me. You are young and un-broken: but, with all this ostentation of your duty, I desire you to show a little more deference to me when I am speaking.

Clarissa, I, xvii

Arguments of this nature occupy the bulk of the first volume of *Clarissa*, and against Clarissa is ranged the whole weight of family authority and precedent—'your father and me and your uncles', not to mention the hostile brother and sister. But all the talk of wills, estates, and marriage settlements which necessarily goes on, doesn't alter the fact that this is a human situation. Here, as in *Pamela*, Richardson draws our sympathy to the isolated individual at the centre of the drama and indicates how Clarissa's desire for the single life is likely to rebound against her. Notice how the single 'I's' beginning the sentences suggest this essential loneliness; a state further suggested by the total absence of family warmth in the meeting. Mrs. Harlowe calls her daughter 'Clary' but the tone is reproving rather than affectionate, and the whole episode implies a one-way only traffic of love flowing between parent and daughter.

If Mrs. Harlowe can intimidate her daughter effectively enough, behind her lurks the dire figure of 'your father'. In the next family confrontation, Mr. Harlowe joins forces with his wife. The weight of their combined oppression can be felt in the very silence of their daughter; a daughter who nevertheless is sensitive enough to feel for her father's gout! Clarissa has been confined to her room and her mother sent to summon her down: as before the episode is described by Clarissa herself in a letter to her friend.

4

Just then, up came my father, with a sternness in his looks that made me tremble. He took two or three turns about my chamber, though pained by his gout. And then said to my mother, who was silent as soon as she saw him :

My dear, you are long absent. Dinner is near ready. What you had to say lay in a very little compass. Surely, you have nothing to do but to declare *your* will, and *my* will—but perhaps you may be talking of the (wedding) preparations. Let us have you soon down—your daughter in your hand, if worthy of the name.

And down he went, casting his eye upon me with a look so stern that I was unable to say one word to him, or even for a few minutes to my mother.

Was not this very intimidating, my dear?

My mother, seeing my concern, seemed to pity me. She called me her good child, and kissed me; and told me my father should not know I had made such opposition. He has kindly furnished us with an excuse for being so long together, said she. Come, my dear, dinner will be upon table presently; shall we go down?—and took my hand.

This made me start : what, madam, go down to let it be supposed we were talking of *preparations*! O my beloved mamma, command me not down upon such a supposition.

You see, child, that to stay longer together, will be owning that you are debating about an absolute duty : and that will not be borne. Did not your father himself some days ago tell you he would be obeyed? I will a third time leave you. I must say something by way of excuse for you : and that you desire not to go down to dinner—that your modesty on the occasion—

O madam! say not my modesty on *such* an occasion : for that will be to give hope—

And design you *not* to give hope? Perverse girl! *Rising and flinging from me*; take more time for consideration! Since it is necessary, *take* more time—and when I see you next, let me know what blame I have to cast upon myself, or to bear from your father for my indulgence to you.

Clarissa, I, xvi

The awesome spectacle of the child (even a child of marriageable years!) in conflict with her parents, clearly fascinated Richardson as much as that of the frightened servant-girl in the power of her master. Here, Clarissa's impossible position is made abundantly clear: she is left daring neither to stay up, in case she is considered merely bashful about marriage, nor to go down in case her family think that she is amenable to their plan. But Clarissa's situation is made even clearer by considering that of her mother: Mrs. Harlowe is plainly fearful of her husband —'silent as soon as she saw him'—and the irony in her trying to persuade Clarissa to an even bleaker marriage prospect with Solmes hardly needs stressing. Like Mrs. Harlowe's 'Clary' earlier, Mr. Harlowe's 'my dear' has a peremptory ring about it, and the way mother and daughter draw closer together after he has left, suggests a mutual need for comfort. The prerogatives of husband/ father are not to be trifled with, and we may note that there are no question marks to *his* queries about what they were doing! Mr. Harlowe, of course, has right as well as power on his side, and if he behaves like a tyrant this is because he conceives of the father's authority as absolute —see Mrs. Harlowe's remark about Clarissa's 'absolute duty'. We must also register the importance of the family relationship: terms like 'father', 'mother', and 'daughter' carry a stronger emphasis in the Richardsonian scheme than they normally do, and when Mr. Harlowe says to his wife, 'Let us have you soon down—your daughter in your hand, if worthy of the name', he is hinting that Clarissa may lose that precious 'name'. This is the ultimate threat to a dutiful daughter. Later, nothing pains Clarissa as much as the knowledge that she has broken this vital bond.

Richardson's interest in family complications extends

into *Grandison* where the pathetic secondary heroine, the Lady Clementina is persecuted by her (Catholic) family for her love of the (Protestant) hero Sir Charles Grandison. Jeronymo, Clementina's brother, writes to Grandison describing the family treatment of her.

5

They condemned, in terms wounding to her modesty, her passion for a foreigner, an enemy to her faith; and on her earnest request to see her father, he was prevailed upon to refuse her that favour.

Lady Juliana Sforza, and her daughter Laurana, the companion of her better hours, never see her, but they inveigh against you as an artful, an interested man.

Her uncle treats her with authority; Signor Sebastiano with a pity bordering on contempt.

My mother shuns her; and indeed avoids me: but as she has been blamed for permitting the interview, which they suppose the wrongest step that could have been taken, she declares herself neutral and resigns, to whatever shall be done by her Lord, by his brother, her two sons, and Lady Juliana de Sforza: but I am sure, in her heart, that she approves not of the new measures; and which are also, as I have reminded the Bishop, so contrary to the advice of the worthy Mrs. Beaumont; to whom they begin to think of once more sending my sister, or of prevailing on her to come hither: but Clementina seems not to be desirous of going again to her; we know not why; since she used to speak of her with the highest respect.

The dear soul rushed in to me yesterday. Ah, my Jeronymo! said she, they will drive me into despair. They hate me, Jeronymo—but I have—written to somebody!— Hush! for your life, hush!

She was immediately followed in by her aunt Sforza and

21

her cousin Laurana, and the general; who, though he heard
not what she said, insisted on her returning to her own
apartment.

What! said she, must I not speak to Jeronymo? Ah,
Jeronymo!—I had a great deal to say to you!

I raved; but they hurried her out, and have forbid her
to visit me : they, however, have had the civility to desire
my excuse. They are sure, they say, they are in the right
way; and if I will have patience with them for a week,
they will change their measures, if they find these new
ones ineffectual. But my sister will be lost, irrevocably lost;
I foresee that.

Ah, Grandison! And can you still—but now they will
not accept of your change of religion. Poor Clementina!
Unhappy Jeronymo! Unhappy *Grandison*! I will say. If
you are not so, you cannot deserve the affection of a
Clementina.

But are *you* the somebody to whom she has written?
Has she written to you? Perhaps you will find some oppor-
tunity to-morrow to let me know whether she has, or not.
Camilla is forbidden to stir out of the house, or to write.

Sir Charles Grandison, II, xxxviii

There is less immediacy here than in the earlier passages,
because the account is a second-hand one. Nevertheless, it
is quite clear that Clementina's situation is no less harrowing than Pamela's or Clarissa's. Again we have the same
isolated figure torn between inclination and obligation, and
the same determined opposition insisting upon their 'right
way'. Like her elder sisters, Pamela and Clarissa, Clementina is kept in a state of rigorous solitary confinement and
like them is forced to her pen for relief—'but I have written to somebody!—Hush! for your life, hush!' Despite
minor differences then, the basic ingredients of all three
situations are the same : at the centre of the stage there is

a beautiful and accomplished female and, surrounding her, various threats to her well-being. Her problem is to deal with the situation without compromising her integrity. She may have to face enemies who have strong claims on her loyalty, and may suffer an inner conflict between conscience and desire; no matter what the difficulties, she is isolated and left to work out her own salvation.

Undoubtedly, Richardson succeeds in engaging our sympathies for his hapless heroines, and in portraying a male-dominated world, brilliantly conveys the anxieties and fears of the young woman faced with difficult decisions. But it would be wrong to suppose from this that he is only concerned with the social or domestic situation involved : his imaginative instinct led him to explore the strange contradictions in human nature itself. Consider the following situation in *Pamela*, in which Mr. B. is forcing Pamela to divulge the whereabouts of her private papers (she has in fact stitched them into her underclothes and he suspects as much). The passage might be compared with the more decorously stated encounter between them cited at the beginning.

6

We were standing most of the time, but he then sat down, and took me by both my hands, and said,—'Well said, my pretty Pamela, *if you can help it*! But I will not let you help it. Tell me, are they in your pocket?'—'No, Sir,' said I; my heart up at my mouth. Said he—'I know you won't tell a downright *fib* for the world; but for *equivocation*! no Jesuit ever went beyond you. Answer me, are they in neither of your pockets?'—'No, Sir,' said I.—'Are they not,' said he, 'about your stays?'—'No, Sir,' replied I: 'but pray, no more questions; for ask me ever so much, I will not tell you.'

'O,' said he, 'I have a way for that. I can do as they do abroad, when the criminals won't confess; torture them till they do.'—'But pray, Sir,' said I, 'is this fair or honest? I am no criminal; and I won't confess.'

'O, my girl!' said he, 'many an innocent person has been put to the torture. But let me know where they are, and you shall escape the *question*, as they call it abroad.'

'Sir,' said I, 'the torture is not used in England; and I hope you won't bring it up.'—'Admirably said!' replied he.

'But I can tell you of as good a punishment. If a criminal won't plead with us here in England, we *press* him to death, or till he does plead. And so, Pamela, that is a punishment that shall certainly be yours, if you won't tell without.'

Tears stood in my eyes, and I said, 'This, Sir, is very cruel and barbarous.'—'No matter,' said he; 'it is but like your *Lucifer*, you know, in my shape! And after I have done so many heinous things by you, as *you* think, you have no great reason to judge so hardly of this; or, at least, it must be of a piece with the rest.'

'But, Sir,' said I (dreadfully afraid he had some notion they were about me), 'if you will be obeyed in this unreasonable manner—though it is sad tyranny, to be sure —let me go up to them, and read them over again, and you shall see so far as to the end of the sad story that follows those you have.'

'I'll see them all,' said he, 'down to this time, if you have written so far, or, at least, till within this week.'— 'Then let me go up to see them,' said I, 'and see what I have written, and to what day, to show them to you, for you won't desire to see every thing.'—'But I will,' replied he. 'But say, Pamela, tell me the truth, are they *above*?' I was much affrighted. He saw my confusion. 'Tell me truth,' said he. 'Why, Sir,' answered I, 'I have some-

24

times hid them under the dry mould in the garden; sometimes in one place, sometimes in another; and those in
your hand were several days under a rose-bush in the
garden.'—'Artful slut!' said he, 'what's this to my question? Are they not *about* you?'—'If,' said I, 'I must pluck
them from my hiding-place behind the wainscot, won't
you see me?'—'Still more and more artful,' said he. 'Is
this an answer to my question? I have searched every
place above, and in your closet for them, and cannot find
them; so I *will* know where they are. Now,' said he, 'it
is my opinion they are about you; and I never undressed
a girl in my life; but I will now begin to strip my pretty
Pamela; and I hope I shall not go far before I find them.'

Pamela, I, Journal, pp. 206–7

This is a cat-and-mouse game and Mr. B. appears in a
much more sadistic light than we saw him earlier. But
despite the tendency towards melodrama—Mr. B's 'O, my
girl!', and Pamela's pleading 'pray Sir'—Richardson
creates a psychologically realistic encounter between two
people whose domestic relationship has grown increasingly involved. Feelings run high, and all the talk of torture and pressing is really an elaborate sexual game,
initiated by Mr. B. and resisted by Pamela. Yet there is no
doubt also that she contributes something to this sadistic
entertainment herself: her sweet reasonableness—'the
torture is not used in England' etc.—provides exactly the
response required. Her reasons for entering this game are
by no means clearly specified; does she do so through fear,
or instinctive artfulness? Is she in a sense egging him on?
By stitching her bulky files into her clothing she is surely
asking for trouble! At any rate, the formal relationship
between master and servant (preserved in the form of
address between them) merely adds spice to their deeper
relationship.

There is an element of this 'power game' in most Richardsonian situations. Certainly on one level he is interested in the moral reactions of his cornered heroines, but at a deeper level he shows himself fascinated by the kind of sufferings they undergo; their very helplessness intrigues him. As one of his characters says, 'human nature is a perverse thing', and while Richardson explores the social and domestic conventions of his time, he also contemplates the psychological turmoil beneath. Thus Lovelace (i.e. Loveless), the arch-villain in *Clarissa*, speculates on the nature of cruelty and in so doing, parables the darker side of the Richardsonian situation. He has been thinking about his general designs on Clarissa and communicates them to his friend Belford.

7

I will illustrate what I have said by the simile of a bird new-caught. We begin, when boys, with birds, and, when grown up, go on to women; and both, perhaps, in turn, experience our sportive cruelty.

Hast thou not observed the charming gradations by which the ensnared volatile has been brought to bear with its new condition? How, at first, refusing all sustenance, it beats and bruises itself against its wires, till it makes its gay plumage fly about, and overspread its well-secured cage. Now it gets out its head; sticking only at its beautiful shoulders : then, with difficulty, drawing back its head, it gasps for breath, and, erectly perched, with meditating eyes, first surveys, and then attempts, its wired canopy. As it gets breath, with renewed rage it beats and bruises again its pretty head and sides, bites the wires, and pecks at the fingers of its delighted tamer. Till at last, finding its efforts ineffectual, quite tired and breathless, it lays itself down and pants at the bottom of the cage, seeming to bemoan its cruel fate and forfeited liberty. And after a few days, its struggles to escape still diminishing as it finds it to no purpose to attempt it, its new habitation becomes familiar; and it hops about from perch to perch, resumes its wonted cheerfulness, and every day sings a song to amuse itself, and reward its keeper.

(A reflection he concludes by saying:)

By my soul, Jack, there is more of the savage in human nature than we are commonly aware of.

Clarissa, II, lxxi

Despite the philosophical reflection in the final sentence, there is a relishing of details here—'ensnared volatile', 'beautiful shoulders', 'pretty head and sides', etc.—which suggests a detachment rather that of the 'delighted tamer' than of the moralist. Lovelace is undoubtedly fascinated by the vision of the encaged Clarissa, but is the author any less so? And are we shocked or merely stimulated by the almost caressing tones of the 'speaker'? The sadistic overtones in Lovelace's description ought surely to arouse strong feelings of repugnance in us and, at the same time, a sympathy for Clarissa's sufferings. If the effect is very different, it is probably because Richardson's moral guard is down and he is letting Lovelace run away with him.

Richardson has sometimes been taken to task for siding with his villains whilst professing morality. It is probably truer (and fairer) to suggest that he was intent upon a thorough exploration of the 'savage in human nature', the factor which most complicates the establishment of the harmonious relationships that he loved to contemplate. In the following passage we can see the lighter world of

Grandison Hall where civilised living is ideally realised.
Harriet (Grandison) is writing.

8

We went through all the offices, the lowest not excepted.
The very servants live in paradise. There is room for everything to be in order: everything *is* in order. The offices so
distinct, yet so conveniently communicating—charmingly
contrived!—The low servants, men and women, have laws,
which, at their own request, were drawn up, by Mrs.
Curzon, for the observance of the minutest of their respective duties; with little mulcts, that at first *only* there was
occasion to exact. It is a house of harmony, to my hand.
Dear madam! what do good people leave to good people
to do? Nothing! Every one knowing and doing his and
her duty; and having, by means of their own diligence,
time for themselves.

*(And as Sir Charles walks in aristocratic company through
the estate as described by Mrs. Curzon:)*

To the lord, they (the tenants) will but seem to lift up their
hats, as I may say; or, if women, just drop the knee, and
look grave, as if they paid respect to his quality only: but
to my master they pull off their hats to the ground, and
bow their whole bodies: they look smiling, and with
pleasure and blessings, as I may say, in their faces: the
good women courtesy also to the ground, turn about when
he has passed them, and look after him—God bless your
sweet face! and God bless your dear heart! will they say
—and the servants who hear them are *so* delighted!—
Don't your ladyship (Harriet) see how all his servants love
him as they attend him at table? How they watch his eye
in silent reverence—Indeed, madam, we all adore him; and
have prayed morning, noon, and night, for his coming
hither and settling among us. And now is the happy time!
28

Forgive me, madam; I am no flatterer; but we all say he has brought another angel to bless us.

Sir Charles Grandison, IV, xliii

If we read this as a factual description, we are likely to regard Grandison Hall no more seriously than Cloud-cuckooland. But Richardson and his contemporaries loved to contemplate ideal situations such as this, where the whole machinery of social relationships is perfectly regulated (see *Pamela*, II, lii, for a similar effusion), and we would do wrong to see in this a mere appetite for the sentimental. Grandison Hall, where servants adore their loving masters, and where husbands and wives, parents and children, exist in perfect harmony, must be viewed against the darker background of B-n Hall and Harlowe Place. As a moralist, Richardson certainly liked to hold up an ideal situation for our instruction, but as an explorer of the human situation, he was more than aware of the harsher realities of life.

Character-portrayal

Richardson's concern with moral conflict led him to group his major characters into opposing sides. Thus the exemplary heroines are faced with thoroughly vicious characters and, within each group, there is a certain conforming to type. But Richardson's main achievement in characterisation is that he offers us a double view of his central characters—an external and an internal one—which renders them much more complex and interesting than they would otherwise have been. In the following extracts, we shall examine this method at work.

Here, first of all, are external and eulogistic descriptions of Pamela and Clarissa: note how the essential 'apartness' of the two girls is stressed, hence their value as exemplars to those who surround them.

9

What an example does this dear lady set to all who see her, know her, and who hear of her; how happy they who have the grace to follow it! What a public blessing would such a mind as hers be, could it be vested with the robes of royalty, and adorn the sovereign dignity! But what are the princes of the earth, look at them in every nation, and what they have been for ages past, compared to this lady? who acts from the impulses of her own heart, unaided in most cases, by any human example. In short, when I (Miss Darnford) contemplate her innumerable excellences, and that sweetness of temper, and universal benevolence, which shine in every thing she says and does, I cannot sometimes help looking upon her in the light of an angel, dropped down from heaven, and received into bodily organs, to live among men and women, in order to shew what the first of the species was designed to be.

Pamela, II, lii

As for Clarissa, Miss Howe spends a good twenty pages describing the qualities possessed by her late friend in a letter to Belford. Here are some sample remarks.

10

Her shape was so fine, her proportion so exact, her features so regular, her complexion so lovely, and her whole person and manner so distinguishedly charming, that she could not move without being admired and followed by the eyes of every one, though strangers, who never saw her before . . .

In her dress she was elegant beyond imitation; and generally led the fashion to all the ladies round her, without seeming to intend it, and without being proud of doing so . . .

She was the most graceful *reader* I ever knew. She added, by her melodious voice, graces to those she found in the parts of books she read out to her friends; and gave grace and significance to others where they were not . . .

But if her voice was melodious when she *read*, it was all harmony when she *sang*. And the delight she gave by that, and by her skill and great compass, was heightened by the ease and gracefulness of her air and manner, and by the alacrity with which she obliged.

Nevertheless, she generally chose rather to hear others sing or play, than either to play or sing herself . . .

She had a talent of saying uncommon things in such an easy manner that everybody thought they could have said the same; and which yet required both genius and observation to say them.

Even severe things appeared gentle, though they lost not their force, from the sweetness of her air and utterance, and the apparent benevolence of her purpose . . .

But it was plain, from her whole conduct and behaviour, that she had not so good an opinion of herself, however deserved; since, whenever she was urged to give her sentiments on any subject, although all she thought fit to say was clear and intelligible, yet she seemed in haste to have done speaking. Her reason for it, I know, was twofold; that she might not lose the benefit of other people's sentiments, by engrossing the conversation; and lest, as were her words, she should be praised into *loquaciousness*, and so forfeit the good opinion which a person always maintains with her friends, who knows when she has said enough . . .

In short, she was the nearest perfection of any creature I ever knew. She never preached to me lessons which she practised not herself. She lived the life she taught. All humility, meekness, self-accusing, others-acquitting, though the *shadow* of the fault was hardly hers (ie. her fatal decision to escape from her family with Lovelace), the *substance* theirs whose only honour was their relation to her.

Clarissa, IV, clxviii

Richardson's early readers loved this kind of adulatory sentiment, and these extracts should be compared with those of similar feeling, to be found at large in the later pages of the three novels. In such passages, Richardson is clearly less concerned with a particular analysis of character than with the building up of an ideal image. For example, the very grossness of the phrase 'bodily organs' stresses the fact that at this stage of the novel, the flesh-and-blood Pamela is of much less interest than her moral qualities. A key word here is Miss Darnford's 'contemplate', because we are to regard both heroines as little more than admirable symbols of womanhood, and the tone throughout is (blatantly) instructive. As befits the eulogy, the writing is expansive and elegant in style, but like most eulogies tells us nothing of vital interest about the two women—Clarissa's graceful reading and singing, for example, scarcely affect the judgment we have already made about her. In effect, both characters as living creatures have disappeared among the hyperbolic utterance they excite and, if we grant that Clarissa is in fact dead and deserves such a monument, can we seriously feel that Pamela is any less so?

Richardson's heroines would be extremely dull figures if we had no other means of knowing them. Apart from these contemplations, however, Richardson offers us a much more intimate knowledge of them through their private letters. As we know, confidential writing is thoroughly revealing and, as the heroines—who are highly impressionable and often in frightening situations—write about their experiences to those in whom they can confide, they produce fascinating self-portraits.

Against the above portrait of Pamela, for example, let us place this earlier extract from one of her letters home. Note particularly the difference between the almost oratorical style of the former and this spontaneous—almost garbled—personal account.

II

DEAR FATHER AND MOTHER,

I shall write as long as I stay, though I shall have nothing but silliness to write; for I know you divert yourselves on nights with what I write, because it is mine. John tells me how much you long for my coming; but he says, he told you he hoped something would happen to hinder it.

I am glad you did not tell him the occasion of my coming away; for *if* my fellow-servants should guess, it were better so, than to have it from you or me; besides, I really am concerned that my master should cast away a thought upon such a poor creature as me; for, besides the disgrace, it has quite turned his temper; and I begin to believe what Mrs. Jervis told me, that he likes me, and can't help it; and yet strives to conquer it, and so finds no way but to be cross to me.

Don't think me presumptuous and conceited; for it is more my concern than my pride to see such a gentleman so demean himself, and lessen the regard he used to have in the eyes of all his servants, on my account.—But I am to tell you of my new dress to-day.

And so when I had dined, up stairs I went, and locked myself up in my little room. There I dressed myself in my new garb, and put on my round-eared ordinary cap, but with a green knot, my home-spun gown and petticoat, and plain leather shoes, but yet they are what they call Spanish leather; and my ordinary hose, ordinary I mean to what I have been lately used to, though I should think good yarn may do very well for every day, when I come home. A plain muslin tucker I put on, and my black silk necklace, instead of the French necklace my lady gave me; and put the ear-rings out of my ears. When I was quite equipped, I took my straw hat in my hand, with its two blue strings, and looked in the glass, as proud as anything. To say truth, I never liked myself so well in my life.

34

O the pleasure of descending with ease, innocence, and resignation!—Indeed there is nothing like it! An humble mind, I plainly see, cannot meet with any very shocking disappointment, let Fortune's wheel turn round as it will.

So I went down to look for Mrs. Jervis, to see how she liked me. I met, as I was upon the stairs, our Rachel, who is the housemaid; she made me a low curtsey, and I found did not know me. I smiled, and went to the housekeeper's parlour: there sat good Mrs. Jervis at work, making a shift: and, would you believe it? She did not know me at first; but rose up, pulled off her spectacles, and said, 'Do you want *me* forsooth?' I could not help laughing, and said, 'Hey-day! Mrs. Jervis, what, don't you know me?' She stood all in amaze, and looked at me from top to toe: 'Why, you surprise me,' said she. 'What, Pamela! thus metamorphosed! How came this about?'

(And when Mr. B. sees her, after first pretending that she is someone else, he angrily rounds on her:)

'Come in,' said he, 'you little villain!' for so he called me. Good Sirs, what a name was there! 'Who is it you put your tricks upon? I was resolved never to honour your unworthiness,' said he, 'with so much notice again; and so you must disguise yourself to attract me, and yet pretend, like a hypocrite as you are—'

I was out of patience then: 'Hold, good Sir,' said I; 'don't impute disguise and hypocrisy to me, above all things: for I hate them both, mean as I am. I have put on no disguise.' —'What a plague,' said he, for that was his word, 'do you mean then by this dress?'—'Why, and please your honour,' said I, 'I mean one of the honestest things in the world. I have been in disguise, indeed, ever since my good lady your mother took me from my poor parents. I came to her ladyship so poor and mean, that these clothes I have on are a princely suit to those I had then: and her goodness heaped upon me rich clothes, and other bounties: and as I am now

35

returning to my poor parents again so soon, I cannot wear those good things without being hooted at: and so have bought what will be more suitable to my degree, and be a good holiday-suit too, when I get home.'

Pamela, I, xxiv

In reading this letter, we not only see Pamela as she appears to the others (Mrs. Jervis, Mr. B., etc.), but also something of her secret life which is hidden from them: her (very natural) delight, for example, in the flattery she receives; her pride in the figure she cuts—'looked in the glass, as proud as anything', 'I never liked myself so well in my life', and so on. In effect, we catch her at an unguarded moment and in setting pen to paper up in her little room, she lets her 'silliness' run on unchecked in a thoroughly revealing and engaging manner. This girlish naïvety displays the real Pamela to us, even to the pride in her 'humble mind'! But when she appears in front of Mr. B., she assumes an instinctive guardedness and we see Pamela in her public role. Her indignation that he should suspect her of trying to allure him is sincerely felt, yet her explanation doesn't entirely tally with the feelings unwittingly revealed to us earlier. She delights in the impression she makes, but is surprised that Mr. B. finds her appearance highly provocative and that he doubts the sincerity of her explanation. As privileged spectators of these discrepancies between Pamela's private and public self, we can guess before she can the source of her confusion: a confusion which ends only with her own realisation that she is in love with Mr. B. and that while she has always said what she meant, she has only partially known her own mind on the subject.

In much the same way that Pamela opens her mind in her letters (and single extracts hardly do justice to the continuous process), so Clarissa, in her correspondence with Miss Howe, reveals feelings which she keeps close from her family. Faced with a forced marriage to Solmes, she writes in desperation to Lovelace who offers protection to her (in the name of his family), requesting that he meet her with transport at the garden gate. She informs Miss Howe of this.

12

This was the purport of what I wrote; and down into the garden I slid with it in the dark, which at another time I should not have had the courage to do; and deposited it, and came up again unknown to anybody.

My mind so dreadfully misgave me when I returned, that to divert in some measure my increasing uneasiness, I had recourse to my private pen; and in a very short time ran (to) this length.

And now, that I am come to this part, my uneasy reflections begin again to pour in upon me. Yet what can I do? I believe I shall take it back again the first thing I do in the morning—yet what *can* I do?

And who knows but they may have a still earlier (wedding) day in their intention, than that which will too soon come?

I hope to deposit this early in the morning for you, as I shall return from resuming my letter, if I do resume it, as my *inwardest* mind bids me.

Although it is now near two o'clock, I have a good mind to slide down once more, in order to take back my letter. Our doors are always locked and barred up at eleven; but the seats of the lesser hall windows being almost even with the ground without, and the shutters not difficult to open, I could easily get out.

Yet why should I be thus uneasy, since, should the letter

go, I can but hear what Mr. Lovelace says to it? His aunts
live at too great a distance for him to have an immediate
answer from them; so I can scruple going to them till I
have invitation. I can *insist* upon one of his cousins meeting me, as I have hinted, and accompanying me in the
chariot; and he may not be able to obtain that favour from
either of them. Twenty things may happen to afford me a
suspension at least: why should I be so very uneasy?—
when likewise I can take back my letter early, before it is
probable he will have the thought of finding it there. Yet
he owns he spends three parts of his days, and has done
for this fortnight past, in loitering about sometimes in one
disguise, sometimes in another, besides the attendance given
by his trusty servant when he himself is not *in waiting*, as
he calls it.

But these strange forebodings! Yet I can, if you advise,
cause the chariot he shall bring with him to carry me
directly for town, whither in my London scheme, if you
were to approve it, I had proposed to go: and this will
save you the trouble of procuring for me a vehicle; as well
as prevent any suspicion from your mother of your contributing to my escape.

But, solicitous for your advice, and approbation too, if
I *can* have it, I will put an end to this letter.

Adieu, my dearest friend, adieu!

Clarissa, I, lxxxiii

(And, an hour or so later, she again writes to her friend:)

13

I went to bed at about half an hour after two. I told the
quarters till five; after which I dropped asleep, and awaked
not till past six, and then in great terror, from a dream,
which has made such an impression upon me that, slightly
as I think of dreams, I cannot help taking this opportunity
to relate it to you.

'Methought my brother, my Uncle Antony, and Mr. Solmes, had formed a plot to destroy Mr. Lovelace; who discovering it, and believing I had a hand in it, turned all his rage against me. I thought he made them all fly into foreign parts upon it; and afterwards seizing upon me, carried me into a churchyard; and there, nothwithstanding all my prayers and tears, and protestations of innocence, stabbed me to the heart, and then tumbled me into a deep grave ready dug, among two or three half-dissolved carcasses; throwing in the dirt and earth upon me with his hands, and trampling it down with his feet.'

I awoke in a cold sweat, trembling, and in agonies; and still the frightful images raised by it remain upon my memory.

But why should I, who have such *real* evils to contend with, regard imaginary ones? This, no doubt, was owing to my disturbed imagination; huddling together wildly all the frightful ideas which my aunt's communications and discourse, my letter to Mr. Lovelace, my own uneasiness upon it, and the apprehensions of the dreaded Wednesday furnished me with.

Clarissa, I, lxxxiv

This is a much more convincing figure than the stereotype of Miss Howe's eulogy. Isolated from friends, and fearful about the consequences of her clandestine letter to Lovelace, Clarissa lets her pen race on in the Pamelaesque manner, running from 'yet' to 'but' to 'if' in a state of tremulous anxiety. Like Pamela also, Clarissa is not so much writing to her friend in the normal way, as writing out of the need to express and release her problems—'to divert . . . my increasing uneasiness, I had recourse to my private pen'. In so doing, she brings her 'inwardest' mind to the surface, divulging both the struggle between her sense of propriety (she knows she ought to 'resume' the fatal letter) and her instinct to escape, and her sense of utter helplessness, as expressed in startlingly naked form by her dream. The dream, with its Freudian stabbings and deep graves, offers us a glimpse of a dark fantasy world, a world which threatens to impair the rational judgments of the virtuous heroine. By endowing Clarissa with this emotional self, Richardson adds a psychological dimension to his heroine, and something very like a 'real life' character appears.

In a private letter, Richardson confided to Sarah Chapone: 'I had no Apprehension so strong, when I was writing the History of Clarissa, as that I should make her Character too perfect to be natural' (*Letters*, p. 206). Like Pamela, Clarissa is saved from unnatural righteousness by the intensity of her emotional life, and like Pamela again, finds the rakish figure who threatens her secretly fascinating: he represents the unlawful champion of her rights who (in the dream) puts the horrid Solmes to flight! Thus, while she consciously deplores his libertine reputation, she nevertheless conducts an illicit correspondence with him and encourages him to protect her against her family. This is how she writes about him to her confidante Miss Howe. Her ambivalent attitude is made quite clear.

14

I have another letter from Mr. Lovelace. I opened it with the expectation of its being filled with bold and free complaints, on my not writing to prevent his two nights watching, in weather not extremely agreeable. But, instead of complaints, he is 'full of tender concern lest I may have been prevented by indisposition, or by the closer confinement which he has frequently cautioned me that I may expect.'

He says, 'he had been in different disguises loitering about our garden and park wall, all the day on Sunday last; and all Sunday night was wandering about the coppice, and near the back door. It rained; and he has got a great cold, attended with feverishness, and so hoarse, that he has almost lost his voice.'

Why did he not flame out in his letter? Treated as I am treated by my friends, it is dangerous for me to lie under the sense of an obligation to any one's patience, when that person suffers in health for my sake.

'He had no shelter, he says, but under the great overgrown ivy, which spreads wildly round the heads of two or three oaklings; and that was soon wet through.'

You remember the spot. You and I, my dear, once thought ourselves obliged to the natural shade which those ivy-covered oaklings afforded us in a sultry day.

I can't help saying I am sorry he has suffered for my sake. But 'tis his own seeking.

His letter is dated last night at eight: 'And indisposed as he is, he tells me that he will watch till ten, in hopes of my giving him the meeting he so earnestly requests. And after that, he has a mile to walk to his horse and servant; and four miles then to ride to his inn.'

He owns, 'that he has an intelligencer in our family; who has failed him for a day or two past: and not knowing how I do, or how I may be treated, his anxiety is increased.'

This circumstance gives me to guess who this intelligencer is: Joseph Leman: the very creature employed and confided in, more than any other, by my brother.

This is not an honourable way of proceeding in Mr. Lovelace. Did he learn this infamous practice of corrupting the servants of other families at the French Court, where he resided a good while?

(And after retailing further points in Lovelace's letter, Clarissa continues:)

I cannot but say, I am sorry the man is not well.

I am afraid to ask you, my dear, what *you* would have done, thus situated. But what I *have* done, I *have* done. In a word, I wrote, 'that I would, if possible, give him a meeting to-morrow night, between the hours of nine and twelve, by the ivy summer house, or in it, or near the great cascade, at the bottom of the garden; and would unbolt the door, that he might come in by his own key. But that, if I found the meeting impracticable, or should change my mind, I would signify as much by another line; which he must wait for until it were dark.'

Tuesday, Eleven o'clock.

I am just returned from depositing my billet. How diligent is this man! It is plain he was in waiting: for I had walked but a few paces, after I had deposited it, when, my heart misgiving me, I returned, to have taken it back, in order to reconsider it as I walked, and whether I should, or should not, let it go. But I found it gone.

In all probability there was but a brick wall, of a few inches thick, between Mr. Lovelace and me, at the very time I put the letter under the brick!

I am come back dissatisfied with myself. But I think, my dear, there can be no harm in meeting him. If I do *not*, he may take some violent measures. What he knows of the treatment I meet with in malice to him, and with a view to frustrate all his hopes, may make him desperate. His behaviour last time I saw him, under the disadvantages of time and place, and surprised as I was, gives me no apprehension of anything but discovery. What he requires is not unreasonable, and cannot affect my future choice and determination : it is only to assure him from my own lips, that I will never be the wife of a man I hate (ie. Solmes). If I have not an opportunity to meet without hazard or

42

detection, he must once more bear the disappointment. All his trouble, and mine too, is owing to his faulty character.

This, although I hate tyranny and arrogance in all shapes, makes me think less of the risks he runs, and the fatigues he undergoes, than otherwise I should do; and still less, as my sufferings (derived from the same source) are greater than his.

Clarissa, I, lxii

Again, there are in effect, two dialogues here: one self-consciously conducted with Miss Howe, friend to friend, the other a kind of self-dialogue where Clarissa, musing about Lovelace, is only half aware of her correspondent. This self-communing punctuates the entire piece—for example, 'Why did he not flame out in his letter?', the repetitive 'I cannot but say, I am sorry the man is not well', and the train of thought following her return from depositing the letter, 'How diligent is this man! . . . In all probability there was but a brick wall, of a few inches thick, between Mr. Lovelace and me, at the very time I put the letter under the brick!' One senses here that Clarissa is impressed by Lovelace's sheer determination; impressed, despite her disgust with his 'infamous practices'. Thus, while she rationalises her attitude to Miss Howe—see the penultimate paragraph—and finally even plays down his sufferings, it is plain that she can no longer regard Lovelace simply as the 'bad man' of her family's painting. Loitering, disguised, suffering for her sake, and dangerously near to her day and night, Lovelace might well appear an intriguing figure to the young heroine, and in the accents of this letter, we can sense the fatal overestimation that Clarissa makes of her own 'choice and determination'. Whatever accolades he allows her later, Richardson very skilfully

43

portrays a fallible human being behind the virtuous pen.

If Richardson brings his heroines to life by thinking himself into their situations, he is no less successful in his portrayal of Lovelace, who emerges through his letters a brilliant figure. Mr. B. is viewed only externally in *Pamela*, and remains somewhat indistinct, partly nightmarish, partly merely boorish. In Lovelace, however, Richardson seems to have found a voice for his own virile fantasies, and there is a zest in Lovelace's writing unparalleled elsewhere in the novels. Here, for example, is what he writes to Belford some time after Clarissa's 'elopement' with him:

15

Fate is weaving a whimsical web for thy friend, and I see not but I shall be inevitably manacled.

Here have I been at work, dig, dig, dig, like a cunning miner, at one time, and spreading my snares, like an artful fowler, at another, and exulting in my contrivances to get this inimitable creature absolutely into my power. Everything made for me. Her brother and uncle were but my pioneers; her father stormed as I directed him to storm; Mrs. Howe was acted by the springs I set at work; her daughter was moving for me, and yet imagined herself plumb against me; and the dear creature herself (Clarissa) had already run her stubborn neck into my gin, and knew not that she was caught; for I had not drawn my sprindges close about her—and just as all this was completed, wouldst thou believe that I should be my own enemy and her friend? That I should be so totally diverted from all my favourite purposes, as to propose to marry her before I went to town, in order to put it out of my own power to resume them?

When thou knowest this, wilt thou not think that my

black angel plays me booty, and has taken it into his head to urge me on to the indissoluble tie, that he might be more sure of me (from the complex transgressions to which he will certainly stimulate me, when wedded) than perhaps he thought he could be from the simple sins in which I have so long allowed myself, that they seem to have the plea of habit?

Thou wilt be still the more surprised when I tell thee that there seems to be a coalition going forward between the black angels and the white ones; for here has hers induced her in one hour, and by one retrograde accident, to *acknowledge*, what the charming creature never before acknowledged, a preferable favour for me. She even avows an intention to be mine—mine, without reformation conditions! She permits me to talk of love to her: of the irrevocable ceremony: yet, another extraordinary! postpones that ceremony; chooses to set out for London; and even to go to the widow's in town.

Well, but how comes all this about? Methinks thou askest. Thou, Lovelace, dealest in wonders; yet aimest not at the *marvellous*. How did all this come about?

I will tell thee: I was *in danger of losing my charmer for ever*. She was soaring upward to her native skies. She was got above earth, by means, too, of the *earth-born*: and something extraordinary was to be done to keep her with us sublunaries. And what so effectually as the soothing voice of love, and the attracting offer of matrimony from a man not hated, can fix the attention of the maiden heart aching with uncertainty, and before impatient of the questionable question?

Clarissa, II, liii

Lovelace's exultation is caused by a letter received by Clarissa from her sister, in which she learns that her family have no intention of forgiving her. This, Lovelace realises, will 'have set (him) at least a month forward with her'.

45

But the important thing here is not so much the content of the extract, as its tremendous gusto. Lovelace glories in his contrivances, but glories more in himself as a kind of Faustian figure, controlling the Harlowes like puppets and engaged in a cosmic duel with the daughter—Clarissa vainly trying to soar aloft to her 'native skies', while he, Lovelace, drags her down to sublunary level. The terrifying power which Clarissa accorded Lovelace in her dream, he might well have considered no more than his due! Lovelace's tendency to see events in highly self-flattering terms is simply an expression of his intense egotism; an egotism which is the driving force behind all his activities. The extravagant flourishes of this letter—and one might cite the characteristic heightening of 'manacled' (married), the idiotically obsessive 'dig, dig, dig', the figurative gloating of 'gin' and 'sprindges', and the entire angelic apparatus befitting Lovelace's heroic conceptions—all demonstrate an overriding concern to inflate things till they correspond with private fantasies. Lovelace's designs on Clarissa are pitifully squalid, but there is no doubt that the imaginative energy of his colourful writing creates a fascinating character for us, and no doubt for Richardson also; though the moralist in him registered the disapproval that he had 'met with more Admirers of Lovelace than of Clarissa' (*Letters*, p. 141).

When we come to Sir Charles Grandison, the last of Richardson's major characters, we find a striking difference in his manner of portrayal. Intent upon drawing a figure of unparalleled virtue, Richardson ignores the all-important internal dimension and dehumanises his hero by a process of endless contemplation. Grandison lacks the interest and vitality of the earlier characters, and his utterances unlike theirs are characterised by an extreme impersonality. This detachment may be seen typically enough in the following: Sir Charles is speaking of the evils of duelling to the rakish Sir Hargrave Pollexfen and his friends, who have been highly impressed by what they have heard so far.

16

'Of what use are the laws of society, if magistracy may be thus defied? Were I to accept of your challenge, and were you to prevail against me, who is to challenge you? and if you fall, who him by whose sword you perish? Where, in short, is the evil to stop? But I will *not* meet you. My system is self-defence, and self-defence only. Put me upon *that*, and I question not but you will have cause to repent it. A *premeditated* revenge is that which I will not meet you to gratify. I will not dare to risk the rushing into my Maker's presence from the consequences of an act, which cannot, in the man that falls, admit of repentance, and leaves for the survivor's portion nothing but bitter remorse. I fear not any more the reproaches of men, than your insults on this occasion. Be the latter offered to me at your *peril*. It is perhaps as happy for you as for myself, that I have a fear of an higher nature. Be the event what it will, the test you would provoke me to, can decide nothing as to the justice of the cause on either side. Already you will find me disposed to do you the justice you pretend to seek. For your own sake, therefore, consider better of the matter; since it is not impossible, but, were we to meet, and both survive, you may exchange what you will think a real disgrace for an imaginary one.'

And thus, gentlemen, have I almost syllogistically argued with myself on this subject:

Courage is a virtue;

Inordinate passion is a vice:

Such passion, therefore, cannot be courage.

Does it not then behove every man of true honour to show, that reason has a greater share than resentment in the boldness of his resolves?

And what, by any degree, is *so* reasonable as a regard to our duty?

You called upon me, gentlemen, to communicate my notions on this important subject. I have the more willingly obeyed you, as I hope Sir Hargrave, on the occasion that brought us to this not unhappy breakfasting, will be the better satisfied that it has so ended; and as, if you are so good as to adopt them, they may be of service to others of your friends, in case of debates among them. Indeed, for my own sake, I have always been ready to communicate my notions on this head, in hopes sometimes to be spared provocation; for, as I have owned, I am passionate: I have pride: I am often afraid of *myself*; and the more, because I am not naturally, I will presume to say, a timid man.

Sir Charles Grandison, I, xlix

This well-prepared harangue is characteristic of the Grandison manner. The views about duelling, of course, are Richardson's own, and perhaps the chief trouble with Grandison is that he is never allowed to speak in his own right. His place in the novel is that of the commentator pure and simple, and the mask never slips once to reveal a credible human being. In his dialogue, for example, there are none of the engaging individual touches—asides, pauses, and so on—which make the commentaries of Richardson's other characters so convincing. Everything Grandison has to say has been thoroughly rehearsed with a view to its moral usefulness—'in case of debates'! Dull though he may be, however, Grandison is important from the technical point of view, since he illustrates the danger of creating a character to a preconceived plan. Shocked by the public interest in his own Lovelace, and interestingly enough, in Tom Jones also, Richardson, it seems, was determined to set the record straight with his 'good man'. Conceived on the heroic scale, Grandison never escapes his label, and unlike the heroines, and unlike the arch-villain Lovelace, retains an allegorical quality throughout. Nothing is more irritating than unalloyed nobility (Grandison's faults, such as the pride and the passion mentioned above, are purely gratuitous), and Richardson was forced to his hero's defence almost before the ink was dry (see the concluding note to the novel). All the same, Grandison provides an instructive contrast with Richardson's other major characters, and indicates the strengths as well as the weaknesses of his method.

Setting and atmosphere

The intense experiences of Richardson's heroines stem directly from the situations they are forced into, and surroundings play an important part in generating the frequently oppressive atmosphere of the novels. In both *Pamela* and *Clarissa*, for example, there is a tremendous feeling of close confinement and restriction, where walls and doors seem to conspire with the persecutors to crush the life out of the heroines.

Here, first of all, is Pamela's account of her unsuccessful attempt to escape from Mr. B's house: she has squeezed through a window, thrown some clothes into the pond (to distract her pursuers) and now tries the garden gate which stands between her and freedom. Notice the emphasis upon the size of the obstacles—'great wooden' lock, 'great garden', etc.—which adds to the nightmare quality of the description.

17

I found that I was most miserably disappointed; for the

wicked woman (Mrs. Jewkes) had taken off that lock, and put another on; so that my key would not open it. I tried in vain, and feeling about, I found a padlock, besides, on another part of the door. O then how my heart sunk! I dropt down with grief and confusion, unable to stir or support myself, for a while. But my fears awakening my resolution, and knowing that my attempt would be as terrible for me as any other danger I could then encounter, I clambered up upon the ledges of the door, and upon the lock, which was a great wooden one, and reached the top of the door with my hands; then, little thinking I could climb so well, I made shift to hold on the top of the wall with my hands; but, alas for me! nothing but ill luck! —no escape for poor Pamela!—The wall being old, the bricks I held gave way, just as I was taking a spring to get up; down came I, and received such a blow upon my head, with one of the bricks, that it quite stunned me; I broke my shins and ancle besides, and beat off the heel of my shoes.

(Pamela then drags herself back to the pond contemplating suicide. Finally, she hides herself in an out-house and waits for her 'cruel keepers' to find her.)

It seems Mrs. Jewkes awaked not till day-break; and not finding me in bed, she called me; and, no answer being returned, she relates, that she got out of bed, ran to my closet; and, missing me, searched under the bed, and in another closet, finding the chamber door, as she had left it, quite fast, and the key, as usual, about her wrist. For if I could have got out of the chamber door, there were two or three passages and doors to them all, double-locked and barred, to go through into the great garden: so that, to escape, there was no way, but out of the window I had passed, because the other windows are a great way from the ground.

Mrs. Jewkes was excessively frightened; she instantly

raised the Swiss, and the two maids, who lay not far off; and finding every door fast, she said, 'I must be carried away, as Peter was out of prison, by some angel.' It is a wonder she had no worse thought.

She says, she wept and wrung her hands, and took on sadly, running about like a mad woman, little thinking I could have got out of the closet window, between the iron bars; and indeed I don't know whether I could do so again. But at last finding that casement open, they concluded it must be so; and ran out into the garden, and found my footsteps in the mould of the bed which I dropt down upon from the leads: immediately Mrs. Jewkes, Colbrand, and Nan, went towards the back-door, to see that it was fast; while the cook was sent to the out-offices, to raise the men, and make them get horses ready, to take each a different way to pursue me.

Finding that door double-locked, and padlocked, the heel of my shoe, and the broken bricks, they concluded I was got away by some means over the wall; and then, they say, Mrs. Jewkes seemed like a distracted woman: till at last Nan had the thought to go towards the pond; and there seeing my coat, cap, and handkerchief, in the water, cast almost to the banks by the agitation of the waves, she thought it was me; and, screaming out, ran to Mrs. Jewkes, and said, 'O Madam, Madam! here's a piteous thing!—Mrs. Pamela lies drowned in the pond.'—Thither they all ran; and, finding my clothes, doubted not I was at the bottom: they all, Swiss among the rest, beat their breasts, and made most dismal lamentations.

Pamela, I, Journal, pp. 148–53

In Pamela's description, Mr. B's house resembles Doubting Castle in *Pilgrim's Progress*—beyond one barred door there is always another. The heroine is helpless and frightened, surrounded by high walls on one side and by locked doors on the other; she can neither go forward nor back.

The situation, in fact, is one familiar to us through dreams, where physical objects are heightened and threatening in themselves. The sensation of claustrophobia, of enclosing obstacles, is greatly increased of course, by Pamela's expectation of pursuit: in the background loom the figures of the fearful Mrs. Jewkes and Colbrand, and the entire posse of Mr. B's lackeys. The tangible world of this setting therefore, which seems to conspire against Pamela's escape —the bricks and mortar between her and freedom—is a symbolic expression of her moral predicament. This is Mr. B's domain, and try as she will, she cannot (and never does) escape from it. Although Mr. B. doesn't appear on the scene, his presence is nevertheless felt not only in Pamela's headlong fear, but also in the distracted antics of Mrs. Jewkes. In fact, we can say that his presence is the more felt in that he doesn't appear, and by a kind of pathetic fallacy, even the pond is 'agitated'! The total setting, then, takes account of things both physical and emotional: Pamela is encircled by walls; behind her stands Mrs. Jewkes; behind Mrs. Jewkes stands Mr. B., and there in tableau form, we have Pamela's situation.

In *Clarissa*, a similar symbolic power is given to setting, except that here Richardson takes the idea of individual confinement further than in *Pamela*. Like Pamela, Clarissa is kept close prisoner in Harlowe Place, but whereas Pamela's escape would have taken her to freedom, Clarissa finds an even worse fate beyond the garden wall: inside Harlowe Place are the hostile family, while outside Lovelace lies in waiting; a reversal of the *Pamela* situation. In this extract, Clarissa is arranging a secret meeting with him, for reasons we have earlier discussed.

A strange diligence in this man! He *says* he almost lives upon the place; and I think so too.

He mentions, as you will see in his letter, four several disguises, which he put on in one day. It is a wonder, nevertheless, that he has not been seen by some of our tenants: for it is impossible that any disguise can hide the gracefulness of his figure. But this is to be said, that the adjoining grounds being all in our hands, and no common footpaths near that part of the garden, and through the park and coppice, nothing can be more bye and unfrequented.

Then they are less watchful, I believe, over my garden walks, and my poultry visits, depending, as my aunt hinted, upon the bad character they have taken so much pains to fasten upon Mr. Lovelace. This, they think (and *justly* think), must fill me with doubts. And then the regard I have hitherto had for my reputation is another of their securities. Were it not for these two they would not surely have used me as they have done; and at the same time left me the opportunities which I have several times had to get away, had I been disposed to do so: and indeed their dependence on both these motives would have been well founded, had they kept but tolerable measures with me.

Then, perhaps, they have no notion of the back door; as it is seldom opened, and leads to a place so pathless and lonesome. If not, there *can* be no other way to escape (if one would) unless by the plashy lane, so full of springs, by which your servant reaches the solitary wood-house; to which lane one must descend from a high bank that bounds the poultry-yard. (This is where Clarissa's letters to Anna Howe are hidden.) For, as to the front way, you know, one must pass through the house to that, and in sight of the parlours and the servants' hall; and then have the open courtyard to go through, and, by means of the iron gate, be full in view, as one passes over the lawn, for a quarter of a mile together; the young plantations of elms and limes affording yet but little shade or covert.

The ivy summer-house is the most convenient for this heart-affecting purpose, of any spot in the garden, as it is not far from the back door, and yet in another alley, as you may remember. Then it is seldom resorted to by anybody else, except in the summer months, because it is cool. When they loved me, they would often, for this reason, object to my long continuance in it: but now, it is no matter what becomes of me. Besides, *cold is a bracer*, as my brother said yesterday.

Clarissa, I, lxxxvi

Along with the incidental information this gives us about the geography of Harlowe Place, its spaciousness and evident wealth, it also apprises us of the world which Clarissa loves and belongs to. Harlowe Place is a world of solid respectability and while it may have become an uncomfortable place for Clarissa of late, it does at least represent the known world to her. Thus, while she details its geographical characteristics in preparation for her escape bid, her words have an import that she is unaware of. Her life so far has been (very contentedly) bounded by the confines of Harlowe Place, but now she contemplates escaping to a largely unknown outside world, in the company of a man whose intentions she has every reason to doubt. When she talks therefore of 'pathless and lonesome' places beyond the 'back door', she unconsciously creates a symbolism about her own situation. Her choice is between Solmes and Lovelace—with the one she may leave Harlowe Place by the front door, with the other, she must resort furtively and irrevocably to the back one: as Lovelace himself cautions later on, 'always be careful of back doors'!

(II, xviii.) In instinctively turning towards the 'shade' and 'covert', Clarissa chances all on Lovelace, and takes the fatal step away from the certainties of her family's world. Like Pamela, Clarissa has no idea what her future will be; she has no idea of just how 'pathless and lonesome' it will prove to be, but to the reader, who can see things in a wider perspective than she can, her descriptive record provides its own revealing allegories.

In passing beyond the boundaries of Harlowe Place, Clarissa simply exchanges one kind of prison for another, and soon afterwards finds herself installed by Lovelace in a London brothel (outwardly a respectable lodging house). In the following passage, Lovelace tells how she begs him to let her leave this dreadful place. The grotesque Mrs. Sinclair, who manages the brothel, typifies the squalid underworld which lies beyond the 'back door' of Clarissa's former existence.

19

Just as she had repeated the last words, *If you mean me honourably, let me go out of this hated house*, in came Mrs. Sinclair, in a great ferment. And what, pray, madam, has *this house* done to you? Mr. Lovelace, you have known me some time; and, if I have not the niceness of this lady, I hope I do not deserve to be treated thus!

She set her huge arms akembo: *Hoh!* madam, let me tell you, I am amazed at your freedoms with my character! And, Mr. Lovelace (holding up, and violently shaking, her head), if you are a gentleman, and a man of honour—

Having never before seen anything but obsequiousness in this woman, little as she liked her, she was frighted at her masculine air, and fierce look—God help me! cried she—what will become of me now! Then, turning her head hither and thither, in a wild kind of amaze, Whom have I for a protector! What will become of me now!

I will be your protector, my dearest love! But indeed you are uncharitably severe upon poor Mrs. Sinclair! Indeed you are! She is a gentlewoman born, and the relict of a man of honour; and though left in such circumstances as oblige her to let lodgings, yet would she scorn to be guilty of a wilful baseness.

I hope so—it may be so—I may be mistaken—but—but there is no crime, I presume, no treason, to say I don't like her house.

The old dragon straddled up to her, with her arms kemboed again, her eyebrows erect, like the bristles upon a hog's back, and, scowling over her shortened nose, more than half hid her ferret eyes. Her mouth was distorted. She pouted out her blubber-lips, as if to bellows up wind and sputter into her horse-nostrils; and her chin was curdled, and more than usually prominent with passion.

With two *hoh-madams* she accosted the frighted fair one; who, terrified, caught hold of my sleeve.

I feared she would fall into fits; and, with a look of indignation, told Mrs. Sinclair that these apartments were mine; and I could not imagine what she meant, either by listening to what passed between me and my spouse, or to come in uninvited; and still more I wondered at her giving herself these strange liberties.

I may be to blame, Jack, for suffering this wretch to give herself these airs; but her coming in was without my orders.

The old beldam, throwing herself into a chair, fell a blubbering and exclaiming. And the pacifying of her, and endeavouring to reconcile the lady to her, took up till near one o'clock.

And thus, between terror, and the late hour, and what followed, she was diverted from the thoughts of getting

57

out of the house to Mrs. Leeson's, or anywhere else.
Clarissa, III, xxviii

Mr. B. had Mrs. Jewkes, Lovelace has Mrs. Sinclair, who is a grimmer version of Pamela's keeper. But whereas Pamela's place of confinement is a spacious Lincolnshire mansion, the extent of Clarissa's degradation is measured by the increasing squalor of her surroundings: surroundings of which the frightful ugliness of Mrs. Sinclair is an integral part. The gracious world which Clarissa once knew is past recall, and when she finally manages to escape from Sinclair's, she is arrested for 'debts' owed to the 'hated house', and taken to a place which, in its very sordidness, represents the depths of her humiliation. Belford describes her situation to Lovelace.

20

A horrid hole of a house, in an alley they call a court; stairs wretchedly narrow, even to the first-floor rooms: and into a den they led me, with broken walls, which had been papered, as I saw by a multitude of tacks, and some torn bits held on by the rusty heads.

The floor indeed was clean, but the ceiling was smoked with variety of figures, and initials of names, that had been the woeful employment of wretches who had no other way to amuse themselves.

A bed at one corner, with coarse curtains tacked up at the feet to the ceiling; because the curtain-rings were broken off; but a coverlid upon it with a cleanish look, though plaguily in tatters, and the corners tied up in tassels, that the rents in it might go no farther. The windows dark and double-barred, the tops boarded up to save mending; and only a little four-paned eyelet-hole of a casement to let in air; more, however, coming in at broken panes than could come in at that.

(And after particularising further horrors:)

And this, thou horrid Lovelace, was the bedchamber of the divine Clarissa!!!

I had leisure to cast my eye on these things : for, going up softly, the poor lady turned not about at our entrance; nor, till I spoke, moved her head.

She was kneeling in a corner of the room, near the dismal window, against the table, on an old bolster (as it seemed to be) of the cane couch, half-covered with her handkerchief; her back to the door; which was only shut to (no need of fastenings!); her arms crossed upon the table, the forefinger of her right hand in her Bible. She had perhaps been reading in it, and could read no longer. Paper, pens, ink, lay by her book on the table. Her dress was white damask, exceeding neat; but her stays seemed not tight-laced. I was told afterwards that her laces had been cut when she fainted away at her entrance into this cursed place; and she had not been solicitous enough about her dress to send for others. Her head-dress was a little discomposed; her charming hair, in natural ringlets, as you have heretofore described it, but a little tangled, as if not lately combed, irregularly shading one side of the loveliest neck in the world; as her disordered, rumpled handkerchief did the other. Her face (oh, how altered from what I had seen it! Yet lovely in spite of all her griefs and sufferings!) was reclined, when we entered, upon her crossed arms; but so as not more than one side of it could be hid.

When I surveyed the room around, and the kneeling lady, sunk with majesty too in her white flowing robes (for she had not on a hoop) spreading the dark, though not dirty, floor, and illuminating that horrid corner; her linen beyond imagination white, considering that she had not been undressed ever since she had been here; I thought my concern would have choked me.

Clarissa, III, cvi

Clarissa's imprisonment in this 'horrid hole' sets the seal upon a career in which her freedom has been progressively narrowed. Her confinement here is (painfully enough) symbolic once more of her predicament, and, one feels, the inevitable outcome of her decision to throw herself upon Lovelace's protection. Let those who trust themselves to back doors beware! At the same time, however, another quite different atmosphere is evoked by Belford's description, and phrases like 'divine Clarissa', 'illuminating that horrid corner', and 'her linen beyond imagination white', suggest the personal triumph over squalid circumstance and indicate the changing mood of the novel. From now on, the heroine's presence increasingly dominates the setting and generates an atmosphere of calm serenity. In the following passage, Clarissa is described in her final earthly lodgings: note the change in atmosphere from the tense bafflement of the earlier scenes to the peacefulness of this tableau described by Belford.

21

We beheld the lady in a charming attitude. Dressed, as I told you before, in her virgin white, she was sitting in her elbow-chair, Mrs. Lovick close by her in another chair, with her left arm round her neck, supporting it, as it were; for, it seems, the lady had bid her do so, saying she had been a mother to her, and she would delight herself in thinking she was in her mamma's arms; for she found herself drowsy; perhaps, she said, for the last time she should ever be so.

One faded cheek rested upon the good woman's bosom, the kindly warmth of which had overspread it with a faint, but charming flush; the other paler and hollow, as if already iced over by death. Her hands, white as the lily, with her meandering veins more transparently blue than ever I had seen even hers (veins so soon, alas! to be choked up by the congealment of that purple stream which already so languidly creeps rather than flows through them!); her hands hanging lifelessly, one before her, the other grasped by the right hand of the kind widow, whose tears bedewed the sweet face which her motherly bosom supported, though unfelt by the fair sleeper; and either insensibly to the good woman, or what she would not disturb her to wipe off, or to change her posture : her aspect was sweetly calm and serene . . .

Clarissa, IV, cxiii

And with the 'charm' of this exemplary dying scene, compare the following account of Mrs. Sinclair's demise : the juxtaposition of the two is quite deliberately arranged by Richardson. Belford again provides the description.

22

But these were the veterans, the chosen band; for now and then flitted in, to the number of half a dozen or more, by turns, subordinate sinners, undergraduates, younger than some of the chosen phalanx, but not less obscene in their appearance, though indeed not so much beholden to the plastering fucus; yet unpropped by stays, squalid, loose in attire, sluggish-haired, under-petticoated only as the former, eyes half opened, winking and pinking, mispatched, yawning, stretching, as if from the unworn-off effects of the midnight revel; all armed in succession with supplies of cordials (of which every one present was either taster or partaker), under the direction of the busier Dorcas, who frequently popped in, to see her slops duly given and taken.

But when I approached the *old wretch*, what a spectacle presented itself to my eyes!

Her misfortune had not at all sunk, but rather, as I thought, increased her flesh; rage and violence perhaps swelling her muscular features. Behold her, then, spreading the whole tumbled bed with her huge quaggy carcass: her mill-post arms held up; her broad hands clenched with violence; her big eyes, goggling and flaming-red as we may suppose those of a salamander; her matted grizzly hair, made irreverent by her wickedness (her clouted head-dress being half off), spread about her fat ears and brawny neck; her livid lips parched, and working violently; her broad chin in convulsive motion; her wide mouth, by reason of the contraction of her forehead (which seemed to be half lost in its own frightful furrows), splitting her face, as it were, into two parts; and her huge tongue hideously rolling in it; heaving, puffing, as if for breath; her bellows-shaped and variously-coloured breasts ascending by turns to her chin, and descending out of sight, with the violence of her gaspings.

Clarissa, IV, cxxxviii

For an Age fond of moralistic death-bed scenes, both these pieces must have provided immense satisfaction. At every point in the two accounts, there is a sharp contrast between Clarissa's state and Sinclair's: the 'charming attitude' of the one, in her symbolically 'virgin white', the writhing discomfort—note the emphasis upon 'swelling', 'clenched', 'goggling', 'splitting', 'heaving, puffing', etc.— of the other, in her 'clouted head-dress'. The pious atmosphere surrounding Clarissa's dying (perhaps too pious and sentimental? see, for example, the description of her veins tearfully dwelt upon) belongs to a different world from that of Mother Sinclair's which has the reek of brimstone

about it. But an important point would be lost if we regarded both scenes simply as moralistic set-pieces. By leaving Harlowe Place with Lovelace, Clarissa entered Sinclair's
underworld—which exists just below the civilised surface
of eighteenth-century life—and risked commitment to that
way of life. Had she fallen to Lovelace's blandishments, she
would have become one of Sinclair's 'undergraduates' and
merited a hellish end. The two worlds therefore (Clarissa's
and Sinclair's) must be seen in relation to each other rather
than as distinct entities, and when we regard the heroine
reclining in Mrs. Lovick's maternal arms, we are put in
mind of that other 'mother' whose 'daughter' Clarissa
almost became.

In the almost plotless *Grandison*, tragic conflict gives
way to social observation and there is little of the balance
and tension between different worlds that we have seen in
Clarissa. True, the novel begins in the *Clarissa* manner with
the abduction of the heroine by a rake, but the merest
glance at the following will indicate the different level of
feeling aroused between Harriet's plight and Clarissa's. Having been carried off from a masquerade (Richardson felt as
strongly about these as about duelling), Harriet describes
how she is then driven away in a coach. Sir Hargrave Pollexfen is the villain.

23

I screamed. Scream on, my dear, upbraidingly, said he; and
barbarously mocked me, imitating, low wretch! the bleating of a sheep—(could you not have killed him for this,
my Lucy?)—Then rearing himself up, Now am I lord of
Miss Byron! exulted he.

Still I screamed for help; and he put his hand before my

mouth, though vowing honour and such sort of stuff; and, with his unmanly roughness, made me bite my lip. And away lashed the coachman with your poor Harriet.

Sir Charles Grandison, I, xxxii

(*Some time later the chariot stops*:)

24

On the chariot's stopping, one of his men came up, and put a handkerchief into his master's hands, in which were some cakes and sweetmeats; and gave him also a bottle of sack, with a glass. Sir Hargrave was very urgent with me to take some of the sweetmeats, and to drink a glass of the wine: but I had neither stomach nor will to touch either.

He ate himself very cordially. God forgive me, I wished in my heart that there were pins and needles in every bit he put into his mouth.

He drank two glasses of the wine. Again he urged me. I said, I hoped I had eaten and drank my last.

You have no dependence upon my honour, madam, said the villain; so cannot be disappointed much, do what I will. Ungrateful, proud, vain, obstinate, he called me.

What signifies said he, showing politeness to a woman who has shown none to me, though she was civil to every other man? Ha, ha, ha, hah! What, my sweet Byron, I don't hit your *fancy*! *You don't like my morals!* laughing again. My lovely fly, said the insulting wretch, hugging me round in the cloak, how prettily have I wrapt you about in my web!

Such a provoking low wretch!—I struggled to free myself; and unhooked the curtain of the fore-glass: but he wrapped me about the closer, and said he would give me his garter for my girdle, if I would not sit still, and be orderly. Ah, my charming Byron said he, your opportunity is over—all your struggles will not *avail* you—Will not *avail* you. That's a word of your own, you know. I will, however, forgive you, if you promise to love me now. But if you stay till I get you to the allotted place; then, Madam, take what follows.

Sir Charles Grandison, I, xxxiii

In essence, Harriet's situation is no less alarming than that of the earlier heroines, and no less than Clarissa before her, she is the helpless fly in the spider's web (see *Clarissa*, III, xxxi, for an identical description). But while Harriet's position may in theory be a desperate one, the reader is never really alarmed for her safety. In the first place, Sir Hargrave, bleating like a sheep or cackling with villainous laughter, is hardly of the Lovelace stature; and nor, for that matter, is Harriet much like the helpless maiden as she curses him with pins and needles. But more importantly, surely, our feelings are not engaged to any great extent because of the retrospective nature of the account. Any kind of dramatic atmosphere which might have emerged is thoroughly deflated by the interpolations—'Could you not have killed him for this, my Lucy?', 'Such a provoking low wretch!', and so on. The language of fear has been overlaid with that of the drawing-room, and Sir Hargrave's villainy, viewed from the safety of the Grandison stronghold, seems merely 'low' or 'provoking'. Harriet, then, is clearly outside her experience, as the other two heroines rarely are when they put pen to paper.

Such retrospectiveness, enabling the kind of reflective commentary that Richardson intended, provides the dominant mood in *Grandison*. Indeed, 'history' is the key word in its title. Harriet herself is soon overshadowed by the Grandison family circle, and her interest in the family and its multifarious activities, together with her particular interest in Sir Charles's marriage intentions, soon turns her active role into a more or less passive one as recorder and commentator. Her letters are therefore informational rather than dramatic; often gossipy and conversational, as Clarissa's never are. This difference in mood may be illustrated again by the following.

25

I will not let you lose the substance of a very agreeable conversation, which we had on Tuesday night after supper. You may be sure, Lucy, I thought it the more agreeable, as Sir Charles was drawn in to bear a considerable part in it. It would be impossible to give you more than passages, because the subjects were various, and the transitions so quick, by one person asking this question, another that, that I could not, were I to try, connect them as I endeavour generally to do.

Of one subject, Lucy, I particularly *owe* you some account. Miss Grandison, in her lively way (and lively she was, notwithstanding her trial so lately over), led me into talking of the detested masquerade. She put me upon recollecting the giddy scene, which those dreadfully interesting ones that followed it had made me wish to blot out of my memory.

I spared you at the time, Harriet, said she. I asked you no questions about the masquerade, when you flew to us first, poor frighted bird! with all your gay plumage about you.

I coloured a deep crimson, I believe. What were Sir Charles's first thoughts of me, Lucy, in that fantastic, that hated dress? The simile of the bird too, was *his*, you know; and Charlotte looked very archly.

My dear Miss Grandison, spare me still. Let me forget that ever I presumptuously ventured into such a scene of folly.

66

Do not call it by harsh names, Miss Byron, said Sir Charles. We are too much obliged to it.

Can I, Sir Charles, call it by *too* harsh a name, when I think how fatal, in numberless ways, the event might have proved! But I do not speak only with reference to that. Don't think, my dear Miss Grandison, that my dislike to myself, and to this foolish diversion, springs altogether from what befel *me*: I had on the spot the same contempts, the same disdain of myself, the same dislike of all those who seemed capable of joy on the light, the foolish occasion.

(After which, Lady L. interjects:)

Indeed, said Lady L., our Harriet's distress has led me into reflections I never made before on this kind of diversion; and I fancy her account of it will perfectly satisfy *my* curiosity.

Sir Charles Grandison, II, iv

Lady L's comment indicates the prevalent interest in *Grandison*—action is considered important in that it provides food for thought. Harriet's own feelings (by now, she is a corporate member of the Grandison family—'our Harriet') are very largely dictated by her new circle, a circle very much of the drawing-room world. Blushes and embarrassment form the chief emotional currency of Harriet's new existence—she frequently colours at the thought of what Sir Charles might be thinking of her—and stronger feelings are much rarer than in the earlier novels. The safe Grandison world has distanced the world of painful experience, and we are never in much doubt that Harriet has 'escaped' as Clarissa never did.

Epistolary technique

We must now consider some of the further aspects of Richardson's letter-writing medium. Perhaps the chief drawback of such a narrative technique is its tendency to run to great length. The letter-writer who aims to be as circumstantial as possible, while at the same time providing a 'talkative' commentary about events, will soon fill a volume. But on the other hand, such a method has certain clear advantages over other narrative methods. Some of these we have already noticed—the way in which, for example, the minds of the letter-writing characters become for us (quite literally) open books. The sensation of actual participation communicated by the confidential letter is undoubtedly the most valuable attribute of the technique, and it is worth re-emphasising the extent to which it enables us to enter the fictional world of the characters. Here, for example, Pamela is writing to her parents about a dreaded interview with Mr. B. Although she is writing about something that has already happened, the actual business of writing recreates the anxious suspense she felt at the time, and this is passed on to her reader.

MY DEAR PARENTS,

I know you longed to hear from me soon; and I send you as soon as I could.

Well, you may believe how uneasily I passed the time till his appointed hour came. Every minute, as it grew nearer, my terrors increased; and sometimes I had great courage, and sometimes none at all; and I thought I should faint when it came to the time my master had dined. I could neither eat nor drink, for my part; and do what I could, my eyes were swelled with crying.

At last he went up to the closet, which was my good lady's dressing-room; a room I once loved, but then as much hated. Don't your heart ache for me? I am sure mine fluttered about like a new caught bird in a cage. 'O Pamela,' said I to myself, 'why art thou so foolish and fearful? Thou hast done no harm! What, if thou fearest an unjust judge, when thou art innocent, wouldst thou do before a just one, if thou wert guilty? Have courage, Pamela; thou knowest the worst! And how easy a choice poverty and honesty is, rather than plenty and wickedness.'

So I cheered myself, but yet my poor heart sunk, and my spirits were quite broken. Every thing that stirred, I thought was to call me to my account. I dreaded it, and yet wished it to come.

Well, at last he rang the bell; 'O,' thought I, 'that it was my passing-bell!' Mrs. Jervis went up, with a full heart enough, poor good woman! He said, 'Where's Pamela! Let her come up; and do you come with her.' She came to me: I was ready to go; but my heart was with my dear father and mother, wishing to share your poverty and unhappiness. I went up, however.

O how can wicked men seem so steady and untouched with such black hearts, while poor innocents stand like malefactors before them!

He looked so stern that my heart failed me, and I wished myself any where but there, though I had before been summoning up all my courage.

'Good heaven,' said I to myself, 'give me courage to stand before this naughty master! O soften him, or harden me!'

'Come in, fool!' said he, angrily, (and snatched my hand with a pull;) 'you may well be ashamed to see me after your noise and nonsense, and exposing me as you have done.'—'I ashamed to see *you*!' thought I: 'very pretty, indeed!' But I said nothing.

'Mrs. Jervis,' said he, 'here you are both together. Do you sit down; but let her stand, if she will.'—'Aye,' thought I, 'if I *can*;' for my knees beat one against the other.

Pamela, I, xvi

As narrative this is extremely slow-moving, but as a reflector of Pamela's feelings as she waits to see what her master will do, it is very effective. All that Pamela dare not say out aloud finds its way into the letter to her parents, and in her unspoken self-dialogue—all the 'said I' and 'thought I' asides—we feel both the depth of her feelings and the extent of the power that Mr. B. wields over her. In the event, the interview proves to be less terrible than she imagined, but in the actual writing of the letter there is a minute by minute re-living of the experience of waiting. By conveying this both to her parents and to the reader (one can imagine what the parents must also be feeling, miles away from their frightened daughter), she conveys to the full the desperate nature of her situation. The subjective account, then, is all-important in this communication; think how much would have been lost if Mrs. Jervis, for example, had provided the account.

A similar epistolary effectiveness can be seen in the next extract where Clarissa is likewise writing for relief. Notice once again the sense of immediacy conveyed by the letter.

27

I was sent for down to tea. I went with a very cheerful aspect; but had occasion soon to change it.

Such a solemnity in everybody's countenance! My mother's eyes fixed upon the tea-cups, and when she looked up it was heavily, as if her eyelids had weights upon them, and then not to me. My father sat half-aside in his elbow-chair, that his head might be turned from me; his hands clasped, and waving, as it were, up and down; his fingers, poor dear gentleman! in motion, as if angry to the very ends of them. My sister sat swelling. My brother looked at me with scorn, having measured me, as I may say, with his eyes as I entered, from head to foot. My aunt was there and looked upon me as if with kindness restrained, bending coldly to my compliment to her as she sat; and then cast an eye first on my brother, then on my sister, as if to give the reason (so I am willing to construe it) of her unusual stiffness. Bless me, my dear! that they should choose to intimidate rather than invite a mind, till now not thought either unpersuadable or ungenerous!

I took my seat. Shall I make tea, madam, to my mother? I always used, you know, my dear, to make tea.

No! A very short sentence, in one very short word, was the expressive answer. And she was pleased to take the canister in her own hand.

My brother bid the footman who attended leave the room. I, said he, will pour out the water.

My heart was up at my mouth. I did not know what to do with myself. What is to follow? thought I.

Just after the second dish, out stepped my mother.—A word with you, sister Hervey! taking her in her hand. Presently my sister dropped away. Then my brother. So I was left alone with my father.

He looked so very sternly that my heart failed me as twice or thrice I would have addressed myself to him; nothing but solemn silence on all hands having passed before.

At last, I asked if it were his pleasure that I should pour him out another dish?

He answered me with the same angry monosyllable which I had received from my mother before, and then arose and walked about the room. I arose too, with intent to throw myself at his feet, but was too much overawed by his sternness even to make such an expression of my duty to him as my heart overflowed with.

Clarissa, I, viii

In describing her own feelings of the time, Clarissa involves the reader in the same sensations of mingled fear and love—sensations, it should be noted, which have a cumulative effect built up over several letters. We see events through Clarissa's eyes, exactly as we saw them through Pamela's earlier, and in each case there is no authorial intrusion to distract us. The way each girl describes things, therefore, is of great importance to our understanding of the total situation. Very little in fact 'happens' in this family encounter, but there is a striking contrast between the almost 'monosyllabic' event and the highly 'expressive' account. Denied any outlet for her feelings among her family, Clarissa, like Pamela before her, finds the release she needs in the letters she can send away. The description of the event, in this case, is eked out with confidential asides to Miss Howe—see the strictly superfluous 'Bless me, my dear!' and 'I always used, you know, my dear, to make tea', where the effect is one of simple overflowing. The actual shape of the letter then is determined by Clarissa's state of mind and, indeed, each of the letters she writes is a similarly faithful dramatisation of her experience.

The advantages of such direct reporting are abundantly clear. But in his first novel, Richardson encountered at least two problems connected with the solely first-hand epistolary account. In the first place, the purely subjective viewpoint, such as Pamela offers us, sometimes narrows the focus too much. And secondly, of course, the single narrator has impossible demands made upon her, for she must write at all times and in all situations in order to keep the story going. In *Clarissa*, Richardson counters these limitations by having two main sets of correspondence, thereby offering us four separate but supplementing narrators. Thus the rigorously subjective keynote of Pamela's narrative is avoided in *Clarissa*, and Clarissa's own viewpoint (and the reader's) is balanced by what Lovelace, for example, has to say. This enlarging of the general viewpoint may be seen from the following extract from a Lovelace letter. Bear in mind that Lovelace's letter comes at a time when we have been fairly committed to Clarissa's point of view by her own revelations to Miss Howe.

28

As to my CLARISSA, I own that I hardly think there ever was such an angel of a woman. But has she not, as above, already taken steps which she herself condemns? Steps which the world and her own family did not think her *capable* of taking? And for which her own family will not forgive her?

Nor think it strange that I refuse to hear anything pleaded in behalf of a standard virtue from *high provocations*. 'Are not provocations and temptations the tests of virtue? A standard virtue must not be allowed to be *provoked* to destroy or annihilate itself.

'May not then the success of him who could carry her *thus far*, be allowed to be an encouragement for him to try to carry her *farther*?' 'Tis but to try. Who will be afraid of a trial for this divine creature? 'Thou knowest that I have more than once, twice, or thrice, put to the fiery trial young women of name and character; and never yet met with one who held out a month: nor indeed so long as could puzzle my invention. I have concluded against the whole sex upon it.' And now, if I have not found a virtue that cannot be corrupted, I will swear there is not one such in the whole sex. Is not then the whole sex concerned that this trial should be made? And who is it that knows this lady, that would not stake upon her head the honour of the whole? Let her who would refuse it come forth, and desire to stand in her place.

I must assure thee that I have a prodigious high opinion of virtue; as I have of all those graces and excellences, which I have not been able to attain myself. Every free-liver would not *say* this nor *think* thus; every argument he uses, condemnatory of his own actions, as some would think. But ingenuousness was ever a signal part of my character.

Satan, whom thou mayest, if thou wilt, in this case call my instigator, put the good man of old upon the severest trials. 'To his behaviour under these trials that good man owed his honour and his future rewards.' An innocent person, if doubted, must wish to be brought to a fair and candid trial . . .

To my point: 'What must that virtue be which will not stand a trial?—What that woman who would wish to shun it?'

Well then, a trial seems necessary for the *further* establishment of the honour of so excellent a creature.

And who shall put her to this trial? Who but the man

who has, as she thinks, already induced her in lesser points to swerve?—And this for her *own* sake in a double sense; not only as he has been able to make *some* impression, but as she *regrets* the impression made; and so may be presumed to be guarded against his further attempts.

The situation she is at present in (ie. she has already eloped with Lovelace), it must be confessed, is a disadvantageous one to her; but, if she overcome, that will redound to her honour.

Shun not, therefore, my dear soul, further trials, nor hate me for making them. 'For what woman can be said to be virtuous till she has been tried?'

Clarissa, II, xi

Lovelace's logic is undoubtedly specious, but there is an undeniable charm about his devilry—'ingenuousness was ever a signal part of my character', and so on. The attractiveness of his argument, however, derives mainly from its appearance of detachment, and its position in the scheme of correspondence is important. Practically the whole of the first volume has been concerned with Clarissa's and Miss Howe's correspondence, and we have taken a highly internalised (female) view of events. Now we begin to hear more and more from Lovelace and Belford which gives us an externalised (albeit equally biased) view of Clarissa's plight. It is not so much that we take sides, but that we are alternately swung between different ways of looking at the same thing.

If the male viewpoint counters the female, variations are also achieved between Miss Howe's letters and Clarissa's. After the heartaches of the Harlowe family relationship conveyed in Clarissa's letters, it is refreshing to read of Miss Howe's with her mother and suitor Hickman. Episodes such as the following provide a comic relief to the tensions of Harlowe Place. Miss Howe is describing a coach ride, during which her mother sits smiling at Hickman, while she herself studiously ignores him:

29

Our courtship days, they say, are our best days. Favour destroys courtship. Distance increases it. Its essence is distance. And to see how familiar these men wretches grow upon a smile, what an awe they are struck into when we frown; who would not make them stand off? Who would not enjoy a power that is to be so short-lived?

Don't chide me one bit for this, my dear. It is in nature. I can't help it. Nay, for that matter, I love it, and wish not to help it. So spare your gravity, I beseech you, on this subject. I set not up for a perfect character. The man will bear it. And what need *you* care? My mother overbalances all he suffers: and if he thinks himself unhappy, he ought never to be otherwise.

Then did he not deserve a fit of the sullens, think you, to make us lose our dinner for his parade (Hickman had spent two hours smartening up his coach for the Howes), since in so short a journey my mother would not bait, and lose the opportunity of coming back that night, had the old lady's condition permitted it? To say nothing of being the cause that my mamma was in the glout with her poor daughter all the way.

At our alighting I gave him another dab; but it was but a little one. Yet the manner, and the air, made up (as I intended they should) for that defect. My mother's hand was kindly put into his with a simpering altogether bridal; and with another How do you now, sir?—all his plump muscles were in motion, and a double charge of care and obsequiousness fidgeted up his whole form, when he offered to me his officious palm. My mother, when I was a girl, always bid me hold up my head. I just then remembered her commands, and was dutiful—I never held up my head so high. With an averted supercilious eye, and a rejecting hand, half-flourishing—I have no need of help, sir! You are in my way.

He ran back, as if on wheels; with a face excessively mortified: I had thoughts else to have followed the too gentle touch, with a declaration that I had as many hands and feet as himself. But this would have been telling him a piece of news, as to the latter, that I hope he had not the presumption to guess at.

Clarissa, I, lxv

This is Anna Howe at her liveliest: her clear physical impressions—'all his plump muscles were in motion', 'fidgeted up his whole form', 'ran back, as if on wheels', together with her strong sense of irony—'I just then remembered her commands, and was dutiful'—reveals a writer both intelligent and humorous. As such, her letter provides a delightful contrast with the apprehensive tone of the six (Clarissa's) which precede it. But there is more than basic comic relief in this: Miss Howe's letter is directed to Clarissa and her awareness of 'gravity' and 'chiding' reminds us of that more serious world beyond her own ambit. Thus, while communicating one set of (humorous) attitudes, and the more humorous because letter-writing encourages uninhibited release, her letter also suggests other attitudes that we must take account of.

In *Grandison*, which provides greater scope for the reflective letter than the dramatic one, there is, nevertheless, a certain degree of epistolary balancing. Harriet Byron's letters generally strike a thoughtful note, while

77

Charlotte Grandison's are similar to Miss Howe's in style and attitude. Compare, for example, the next extract with the previous one. Lady G., as Charlotte now is, is indulging her favourite sport of husband-baiting; this time publicly in front of some guests. Her attitude towards her husband provides an obvious contrast to the almost reverential regard Harriet shows for Sir Charles.

30

My lord not coming in, and the dinner being ready, I ordered it to be served.—Won't you wait a little longer for Lord G? No. I hope he is safe and well. He is his own master as well as mine (I sighed, I believed!), and no doubt has a paramount pleasure in pursuing his own choice.

They raved. I begged that they would let us eat our dinner with *comfort*. My lord, I hoped, would come in with a keen appetite, and Nelthorpe should get a supper for him that he liked.

When we had dined and retired into the adjoining drawing-room, I had another schooling-bout: Emily was even saucy. But I took it all: yet in my heart was vexed at Lord G's perverseness.

At last, in came the *honest* man. He does not read this, and so cannot take exceptions, and I hope *you* will not, at the word *honest*.—So lordly! so stiff! so solemn!—Upon my word! Had it not been Sunday I would have gone to my harpsichord directly. He bowed to Lord and Lady L., and to Emily, very obligingly; to me he nodded.—I nodded again; but, like a good-natured fool, smiled. He stalked to the chimney; turned his back towards it, buttoned up his mouth, held up his glowing face as if he were disposed to crow; yet had not won the battle.—One hand in his bosom; the other under the skirt of his waistcoat, and his posture firmer than his mind.—Yet was my heart so devoid of malice, that I thought his attitude very genteel; and, had we not been man and wife, agreeable.

We hoped to have found your lordship at home, said Lord L., or we should not have dined here.—If Lord G. is as polite a *husband* as a *man*, said I, he will not thank your lordship for this compliment to his wife.—Lord G. swelled and reared himself up. His complexion, which was before in a glow, was heightened.

Poor man! thought I. But why should my tender heart pity obstinate people? Yet I could not help being dutiful. —Have you dined, my lord? said I, with a sweet smile and very courteous.

He stalked to the window, and never a word answered he.

Pray, Lady L., be so good as to ask my Lord G. if he has dined? Was this not very condescending on such a behaviour?—Lady L. *asked* him; and as gently-voiced as if she were asking the same question of her own lord. Lady L. is a kind-hearted soul, Harriet. She is *my* sister.

I have *not*, madam, to Lady L., turning rudely from me, and not very civilly from her. Ah! thought I, these men! The more they are courted!—Wretches! to find their consequence in a woman's meekness.—Yet I could not forbear showing mine.—Nature, Harriet! Who can resist constitution?

Sir Charles Grandison, III, xxiii

This is fine example of the sex-war waged continuously by Lady G. against the vile encroachments of the male. She does this somewhat self-consciously here, because she knows that Harriet will certainly not agree with her rough handling of Lord G., however, her real target is husbands in general—'these men!'. But apart from the important connexion this letter has with the ideal marriage theme of the novel, its chief distinction is its 'voice'. Lady G's contemptuous attitude (like Miss Howe's) shows itself in the actual manner of her writing, and in playing off one attitude against another, Richardson alters the epistolary style accordingly. Here Lady G. is not only prepared to ridicule her husband in company, but also (and even less forgiveably) in the letter to Harriet. Thus the embarrassed gestures of Lord G. are parodied in the abrupt and deliberately unseemly phrases of her letter—'buttoned up his mouth', 'held up his glowing face as if he were disposed to crow', and so on—where the very directness and unkindness of her scrutiny is reflected in the adopted style. Similarly, the comic 'swelled and reared himself up', and the dramatically stylised, 'and never a word answered he', show not merely the antics of the 'stiff' husband, but also the ironic detachment of his provoking wife.

In the epistolary novel, then, one is brought to judgments about the characters as much by their writings as by their actions, and Richardson deliberately uses epistolary style as a reflection of character. Thus the termagant spirits of Miss Howe and Lady G. reveal themselves in the characteristic forcefulness of their phrasings, and at least one early critic (Lady Mary Wortley Montagu) denounced Charlotte's 'coarse jokes and low expressions as are only to be heard among the lowest class of people'. Doubtless the kind of phrases we have been considering were uppermost in her mind, but what Lady Mary fails to appreciate, apparently, is that Richardson would certainly have agreed with her.

Lady G. is lively but hardly really objectionable. When a thoroughly unpleasant character appears on the scene, however, Richardson delights in producing an epistolary caricature. The following piece written by Brand, a conceited young clergyman in *Clarissa*, is a fine example of epistolary pomposity exactly matching the pretentiousness of the character behind it. Brand's comic turn occurs at a particularly harrowing part of the novel (just before Clarissa's death) and makes a pointed contrast with it: the seriousness of the letter's content serves to heighten the absurdity of its style.

31

DEAR MR. WALTON,—I am obliged to you for the very handsomely penned (and elegantly written) letter which you have sent me on purpose to do justice to the character of the younger Miss (Clarissa) Harlowe: and yet I must tell you that I had reason, before that came, to think (and to know indeed) that we were all wrong: and so I had employed the greatest part of this week in drawing up an apologetical letter to my worthy patron Mr. John Harlowe, in order to set all matters right between me and them, and (as far as I could) between them and miss. So it required little more than connexion and transcribing when I received yours; and it will be with Mr. Harlowe aforesaid to-morrow morning; and this, and the copy of that, will be with you on Monday morning.

You cannot imagine how sorry I am that you, and Mrs. Walton, and Mrs. Barker, and I myself, should have taken matters up so lightly (judging, alas-a-day! by appearance and conjecture) where character and reputation are concerned. Horace says truly:

Et semel emissum volat irrevocabile verbum.

That is, Words once spoken cannot be recalled: but (Mr. Walton) they may be contradicted by other words; and we may confess ourselves guilty of a mistake; and express our concern for being mistaken; and resolve to make our mistake a warning to us for the future: and this is all that can be done; and what every worthy mind will do; and what nobody can be readier to do than we four undesigning offenders (as I see by your letter, on your part; and as you will see by the enclosed copy on mine); which, if it be received as I think it ought (and as I believe it will), must give me a speedy opportunity to see you, when I visit the lady; to whom (as you will see in it) I expect to be sent up with the olive-branch.

(After several pages more of this, Brand concludes his letter :)

You will perhaps, Mr. Walton, wonder at the meaning of the lines drawn under many of the words and sentences (UNDERSCORING we call it); and were my letters to be printed, those would be put in a different character. Now, you must know, sir, that we learned men do this to point out to the readers who are not so learned where the jet of our arguments lieth, and the emphasis they are to lay upon those words; whereby they will take in readily our sense and cogency.

Clarissa, IV, cvii

Brand's learned pedantry (and Richardson as a printer must have revelled in all that 'underscoring') is at the furthest pole from the ideal qualities of letter-writing which are consistently stressed, not only in *Clarissa*, but throughout Richardson's fiction. Brand's ridiculous elegance, Lady G's and Miss Howe's skittishness, and Lovelace's stylish energy, all provide revealing and entertaining facets of the epistolary medium. But Richardson, despite his evident delight in the various kinds of stylistic exuberance he portrays, takes pains to remind his readers that plainer qualities of writing provide the best indications of sincerity. Comments like the following occurring frequently in the novels and in his own letters, show his concern with what one might call the moral aspect of style:

. . . for, you must know, that what we admire in *you*, are truth and nature, not studied or elaborate epistles. We can hear at church, or read in our closets, fifty good things that we expect not from you: but we cannot receive from any body else the pleasure of sentiments flowing with that artless ease, which so much affects us when we read your letters.

Lady Davers to Pamela, Pamela, II, xii

But you must not expect, madam, that although I have written what I have read to you, I shall approve of it in my observations upon it; for I am convinced, that no style can be proper, which is not plain, simple, easy, natural and unaffected.

Pamela to Miss Stapylton, Pamela, II, cii

This, meantime, I will venture to repeat, is certain, that the style is that truly easy, simple, and natural one, which we should admire in other authors excessively.

Belford commenting upon biblical style to Lovelace,
Clarissa, IV, iii

. . . but why the diffidence to such a one as I am!—a plain writer: a sincere well-wisher: an undesigning scribbler; who admire none but the natural and easy beauties of the pen . . .

Richardson to Sophia Westcomb, Letters, p. 66

Ease, spontaneity and naturalness then are criteria for any kind of writing, but most of all for letter-writing where the temptation to elaborate is greatest. Though the heroines' letters are by no means always free from sophistication of one kind or another, by and large they approximate to Richardson's ideal epistolary standard of naturalness and, read in conjunction with the letters of other characters, serve a thoroughly exemplary purpose. Mr. B., for example, coming upon Pamela's writing is able to compliment not only her honest behaviour, but the corresponding 'easy and happy manner of (her) narrative' (I, Journal, p. 268). Precisely because character and writing are all of a piece, we can arrive at exactly the opposite estimate of a Lovelace or Brand.

The epistolary technique, therefore, furnished Richardson with at least three positive aids to an illuminating presentation of his fictional world. It enabled him to create a high degree of dramatic involvement through the letters written almost on the field of action; it enabled him to vary the tension and focus of narration by the introduction of commentaries coming from a variety of different vantage points (and remember how skilfully Richardson keeps his heroines at a distance from their friends); and finally, it enabled him to establish a scale of values based upon the character-image reflected in letter-writing. When we read the letters of which these novels are composed, we read them not as isolated fragments of narration, but as powerful reflectors of the Richardsonian vision.

Range and achievement

Discussion of Richardson's epistolary technique leads us on to consider the range and achievement of his fiction, for there is no doubt that both are bound up with his talents as a creative letter-writer. Letter-writing clearly came easily to him, and the intimacy of the medium itself offered him opportunities for expansiveness that other narrative methods might well have denied him. With this in mind, in these final selections, we shall be looking at some of the ways he used these opportunities, revealing as he did so, the extent and limitation of his talents.

In the first place, by endowing his major letter-writers with sharp eyes and methodical minds, Richardson was able to achieve a descriptive realism that was at once both authentic of the real, everyday world, and at the same time sharply significant within its own fictional world. This can be seen, for example, in the following scene where, having been told that she can go home, Pamela is sorting out her clothes into bundles, whilst talking to Mrs. Jervis the kindly housekeeper. Pamela is describing the occasion in her usual garrulous fashion, in what she thinks will be perhaps her last letter home.

32

So I said, when she came up, 'Here, Mrs. Jervis, is the first parcel: I will spread it all abroad. These are the things my good lady gave me. In the first place,'—and so I went on describing the clothes and linen my lady had given me, mingling blessings as I proceeded, for her goodness to me: when I had turned over that parcel, I said, 'Well, so much for the first parcel, Mrs. Jervis; that was my lady's gifts.

'Now I come to the presents of my dear virtuous master: hey, you know, *closet* for that, Mrs. Jervis.' She laughed and said, 'I never saw such a comical girl in my life: but go on.'—'I will, Mrs. Jervis,' said I, 'as soon as I have opened the bundle;' for I was as brisk and as pert as could be, little thinking who heard me.

'Now here,' said I, 'are my ever-worthy master's presents;' and then I particularised all those in the second bundle. After which I turned to my own, and said—

'Now comes poor Pamela's bundle: and a little one it is to the others. First, here is a calico night-gown, that I used to wear o' mornings. 'Twill be rather too good for me when I get home; but I must have something. Then, there is the quilted calimanco coat, a pair of stockings I bought of the pedlar, my straw hat with blue strings: and a remnant of Scotch cloth, which will make two shirts and two shifts, the same I have on, for my poor father and mother. And here are four other shifts, one the fellow to that I have on; another pretty good one, and the other two old fine ones, that will serve me to turn and wind with at home, for they are not worth leaving behind me; and here are two pair of shoes; I have taken the lace off, which I will burn, and may-be will fetch me some little matter at a pinch, with an old silver buckle or two.

'What do you laugh for, Mrs. Jervis?' said I. 'Why, you are like an April day; you cry and laugh in a breath.

'Well, let me see: here's a cotton handkerchief I bought of the pedlar; there should be another somewhere. O here it is; and here are my new-bought knit mittens; this is my new flannel coat, the fellow to that I have on: and in this parcel, pinned together, are several pieces of printed calico, remnants of silk, and such-like, that, if good luck should happen, and I should get work, would serve for robings and facings, and such-like uses. Here too are a pair of pockets; they are too fine for me; but I have no worse. Bless me, I did not think I had so many good things.'

Pamela, I, xxix

In this, we can see one of the chief ingredients of Richardson's descriptive realism: his minute particularising of concrete things. Elsewhere, one finds details of furnishings, the lay-out of rooms, near-catalogues of books, china and other domestic items, and the total effect, as here with Pamela's clothing, is to build up a convincing tangible world. But apart from providing a solidly realistic background, this lengthy inventory of Pamela's linen also discloses a world of private feelings. Each of the bundles (and such bundling is one of Pamela's particular domestic virtues) has important associations for her, and clothing itself has a more than ordinary significance in the novel. Thus her lady's (Mr. B's mother) bundle reminds her of earlier and happier days with the B. family; Mr. B's, of attempted bribery and corruption (see the first letters in the novel); and finally her own conjures up the lowly but honest future that lies ahead of her. Pamela's happy soliloquising then—and the more happy because she feels safe among her familiar bundles—presents us with a reassuringly snug domestic scene; a scene all the more reassuring for the presence of Mrs. Jervis. But Pamela's unrestrained chatter about her calicoes and mittens, and her vision of a future free from designing masters is, unknown to her, being listened to by Mr. B. as well as by Mrs. Jervis : Richardson having concealed him in the closet beforehand to savour every word with amorous intent. Thus the innocent cataloguing of linen, hats and shoes enters ears it was not intended for, and as the methodical Pamela reviews her life according to bundle, Mr. B. savours the thought that her future is entirely in his hands. The gratuitous trick of concealing Mr. B. in every available cupboard is an obvious manifestation of Richardson's own prurient interest in his heroine; of his anxiety to keep her under constant espial, especially at unguarded moments such as the above. But at the same time, his interest in the minutest intricacies of feminine activity, together with his ability to capture the authentic tones of Pamela's prattle—'as brisk and as pert as (can) be'—achieves a high degree of actuality.

If Richardson sometimes scrutinises his heroine too closely for comfort, he often compensates by showing us what things look like from her point of view. When Pamela is transferred from the reasonably comfortable world of Mr. B's Bedfordshire estate to Lincolnshire, she finds herself watched over by Mrs. Jewkes and Colbrand, and having no Mrs. Jervis to chatter to is forced to set down her thoughts in a secret journal. This is how she writes about the tongue-tying ugliness of her new larger-than-life warders.

33

Now I will give you a picture of this wretch. She is a broad, squat, pursy, *fat thing*, quite ugly, if any thing human can be so called; about forty years old. She has a huge hand, and an arm as thick as my waist, I believe. Her nose is flat and crooked, and her brows grow down over her eyes; a dead, spiteful, grey, goggling eye, to be sure she has; and her face flat and broad: and as to colour, looks as if it had been pickled a month in saltpetre: I dare say she drinks. She has a hoarse man-like voice, and is as thick as she's long: and yet looks so deadly strong, that I am afraid she would dash me at her foot in an instant, if I was to vex her. So that with a heart more ugly than her face, she frightens me sadly; and I am undone, to be sure, if God does not protect me; for she is very, very wicked—indeed she is.

This is poor helpless spite in me:—but the picture is too near the truth, notwithstanding. She sends me a message, just now, that I shall have my shoes again, if I will accept of her company to walk with me in the garden—To *waddle* with me rather, thought I. (I, Journal, p. 97.)

(And later, Pamela is introduced to Colbrand in a mockery of drawing-room ceremony.)

She (Mrs. Jewkes) said she would go down to order supper, and insisted upon my company. I would have excused myself; but she put on a commanding air, that I durst not oppose. When I went down, she took me by the hand, and presented me to the most hideous monster I ever saw in my life. 'Here, Monsieur Colbrand,' said she, 'here is *your* pretty ward and *mine*; let us try to make her time with us easy.' He bowed, put his foreign grimaces, and, in broken English, told me, 'I was happy in de affections of de vinest gentleman in de varld!' I was quite frightened, and ready to drop down; I will describe him to you, my dear father and mother, and you shall judge if I had not reason to be alarmed, as I was apprised of his hated employment, to watch me closer.

He is a giant of a man for stature; taller by a good deal than Harry Mawlidge, in your neighbourhood, and large-boned, scraggy, and has a hand!—I never saw such an one in my life. He has great staring eyes, like the bull's that frightened me so; vast jaw-bones sticking out; eye-brows hanging over his eyes; two great scars upon his fore-head, and one on his left cheek; two large whiskers, and a monstrous wide mouth; blubber lips, long yellow teeth, and a hideous grin. He wears his own frightful long hair, tied up in a great black bag; a black crape neckcloth, about a long ugly neck; and his throat sticking out like a wen. As to the rest, he was dressed well enough, and had a sword on, with a nasty red knot to it; leather gaiters, buckled below his knees; and a foot near as long as my arm, I verily think.

Pamela, I, Journal, p. 145

There is a strong vein of fantasy in these descriptions, and one which can be found at large in Richardson's por-trayal of wicked characters. Mrs. Sinclair, for example, in *Clarissa* is simply Mrs. Jewkes writ even larger, and the clergyman hired by Sir Hargrave to marry him to Harriet Byron in *Grandison*, bears a remarkable resemblance to Col-brand. The same physical characteristics tend to recur in each case—staring eyes, yellow teeth, huge hands, and so on—and it is quite obvious that each is a variation upon one theme. In equating wickedness with grotesque physical characteristics Richardson is merely drawing upon a well-established literary tradition, but it is also plain that in these portraits the same fantasies are being worked out again and again. Placing himself in the position of a fright-ened and helpless female—frightened that is of physical outrage in the main—Richardson draws a gallery of night-marish grotesques shaped in the way that personally fascinated him. But while we can easily select the absurdly grotesque parts of these descriptions—perhaps, Mrs. Jewkes' eye, or Colbrand's 'blubber lips, long yellow teeth, and (a) hideous grin', and so on (individual readers will find their own choice specimens here)—parts which tend to lift the characters into a fairy-tale context, we should not assume that Richardson allows himself to be mastered by his own fantasies. In the first place, of course, this is how Pamela herself sees her keepers, and, as she admits, her portrait of Mrs. Jewkes is motivated by spite—hence, perhaps, the piling up of vengeful adjectives to describe the eye that watches over her—and that of Colbrand, by fear—'I was quite (i.e., 'absolutely', cf. 'quite ugly' in the Jewkes sketch) frightened'. In the second place, both figures are finally kept within everyday proportions by Pamela's calmer reflections about them. Mrs. Jewkes may be a terrible woman, and do barbarous things like taking Pamela's shoes away from her, but she is less than ogreish in that she probably drinks, is as thick as she is long, and can only muster a 'waddle' (a definite source of comfort to a heroine considering escape!). Similarly, Colbrand may be in all respects a 'hideous monster', but at least he can bow, wears decent clothes, and may perhaps invite comparison for stature with Harry Mawlidge. Small comfort perhaps, but at least these are things belonging to the known world.

The tendency to create monsters, then, is held in check by an attention to everyday detail, and the imagination which is capable of cataloguing Pamela's wardrobe is equally capable of listing the deadly attributes of a Jewkes or Colbrand, in a similarly matter-of-fact way. The strength of this descriptive quality can perhaps be best illustrated from a scene which Richardson laboured to make as shocking as possible; Mrs. Sinclair's death-bed scene laid in her brothel, another part of which we have already quoted in a different context. The sober Belford (increasingly used to provide the Richardsonian commentary) is the writer. Unlike Pamela, he can afford to be quite objective about what he sees.

34

The old wretch had once put her leg out by her rage and violence, and had been crying, scolding, cursing, ever since the preceding evening, that the surgeon had told her it was impossible to save her; and that a mortification had begun to show itself; insomuch that purely in compassion to their own *ears*, they had been forced to send for another surgeon, purposely to tell her, though against his judgment, and (being a friend of the other) to seem to convince *him* that he mistook her case; and that, if she would be patient, she might recover. But, nevertheless, her apprehensions of death, and her antipathy to the thoughts of dying, were so strong that their imposture had not the intended effect, and she was raving, crying, cursing, and even howling, more like a wolf than a human creature, when I came; so that as I went upstairs I said: Surely this noise, this howling, cannot be from the unhappy woman! Sally said it was; and assured me that it was nothing to the noise she had made all night; and stepping into her room before me, Dear *Madam* Sinclair, said she, forbear this noise. It is more like that of a bull than a woman! Here comes Mr. Belford; and you'll frighten him away if you bellow at this rate.

There were no less than eight of her cursed daughters surrounding her bed when I entered; one of her partners, Polly Horton, at their head; and now Sally, her other partner, and *Madam* Carter, as they called her (for they are all *madams* with one another), made the number ten: all in shocking dishabille, and without stays, except Sally, Carter, and Polly; who, not daring to leave her, had not been in bed all night.

The other seven seemed to have been but just up, risen perhaps from their customers in the fore house, and their nocturnal orgies, with faces, three or four of them, that had run, the paint lying in streaky seams not half blowzed off, discovering coarse wrinkled skins: the hair of some of them of divers colours, obliged to the blacklead comb where black was affected; the artificial jet, however, yielding apace to the natural brindle: that of others plastered with oil and powder; the oil predominating: but every one's hanging about her ears and neck in broken curls or ragged ends; and each at my entrance taken with one motion, stroking their matted locks with both hands under their coifs, mobs, or pinners, every one of which was awry. They were all slip-shoed; stockingless some; only under-petticoated all; their gowns, made to cover straddling hoops, hanging trollopy, and tangling about their heels; but hastily wrapped round them as soon as I came upstairs. And half of them (unpadded, shoulder-bent, pallid-lipped, limber-jointed wretches) appearing, from a blooming nineteen or twenty perhaps over night, haggard well-worn strumpets of thirty-eight or forty.

I am the more particular in describing to thee the appearance these creatures made in my eyes when I came into the room because I believe thou never sawest any of them, much less a group of them, thus unprepared for being seen.[1] I, for my part, never did before; nor had I now, but

---

[1] Whoever has seen Dean Swift's Lady's Dressing-room will think this description of Mr. Belford not only more *natural* but more *decent painting*, as well as better justified by the *design*, and by the *use* that may be made of it. (Richardson's footnote as 'editor'.)

upon this occasion, been thus *favoured*. If thou *hadst*, I believe thou wouldst hate a profligate woman, as one of Swift's Yahoos, or Virgil's obscene harpies, squirting their ordure upon the Trojan trenchers; since the persons of such in their retirements are as filthy as their minds—hate them as much as I do; and as much as I admire, and next to adore, a truly virtuous and elegant woman : for to me it is evident, that as a neat and clean woman must be an angel of a creature, so a sluttish one is the impurest animal in nature.

Clarissa, IV, cxxxviii

This passage which contains some of Richardson's best descriptive writing, also provides us with a clear illustration of the limitations imposed by his moral purpose—his concern that we should make good 'use' of the dreadful scene. In the first place, of course, there is the masterly stripping away of the brothel mask : the highly impressive accumulation of disgusting detail—all the paints, powders and plastering oils of female debauchery—in which each new item serves to widen the gap between the false madamish gentility on the surface and the revolting reality underneath. The whole thing is done with a convincing objectivity, even though the effect is suggestive of an allegorical procession in a medieval painting. There are the the deft, realistic touches too, as when on Belford's appearance, all the women automatically smooth their hair—a gesture, which in its purely mechanical nature, sadly sums up their lives. Notice also, the careful attention to numbers—'no less than eight', 'the other seven', etc.—which helps to provide a sense of actuality. But such observation gives way towards the end to a superfluous moralising and allusion-hunting, which, together with Richardson's own footnote intrusion, comes near to undoing the effectiveness of the earlier part. While it may salve Belford's moral indignation to see profligate women as harpies and yahoos, mention of Virgil and Swift really takes us out of the skilfully wrought context of tangible 'unpadded, shoulder-bent, pallid-lipped, limber-jointed' creatures, and places us in a remote mythological world. And the real event becomes even more of a literary occasion when Richardson himself takes up cudgels with Swift in praising Belford's purposeful natural description. By this time we are fully out of Sinclair's world and, indeed, out of the novel itself! Nor perhaps are we much disposed to take notice of a morality which equates personal cleanliness with virtue, and its opposite with vice. As so often in Richardson, the language of strong natural description is reined in by a sober reflectiveness, and the harsh picture that he paints here, tends to be spoilt by the tag underneath.

Spoilt, that is, according to twentieth-century taste, but we must remember that Richardson's Age valued the retailing of unpleasant facts chiefly for the reflection they inspired—this was their justification for realism. We must also remember the different emotional temper of the Age, and Richardson is equally prepared to draw tears as well as disgust by his scene painting. The same remorseless intent to describe all, to let nothing escape his prying eye, can be seen in his depiction of pathetic scenes, of which there are a large number in his novels. This kind of writing is really a branch of the descriptive realism we have been considering, where ugliness—rape or death—is refined by the tragic sense awakened in the spectators. Far from being a flinching away from the unpleasantly realistic, scenes like the following show a gruesome concentration upon it. Colonel Morden, Clarissa's cousin, in a series of lengthy letters to Belford is giving a moment by moment account of the funeral solemnities following upon Clarissa's arrival back to Harlowe Place in her coffin. At this point she has been dead about four days.

35

When the unhappy mourners were all retired, I directed the lid of the coffin to be unscrewed, and caused some fresh aromatics and flowers to be put into it.

The corpse was very little altered, notwithstanding the journey. The sweet smile remained.

The maids who brought the flowers were ambitious of strewing them about it: they poured forth fresh lamentations over her; each wishing she had been so happy as to have been allowed to attend her in London. One of them particularly, who is it seems, my Cousin Arabella's personal servant, was more clamorous in her grief than any of the rest; and the moment she turned her back, all the others allowed she had reason for it. I inquired afterwards about her, and found that this creature was set over my dear cousin when she was confined to her chamber by indiscreet severity.

Good Heaven! that they should treat, and suffer thus to be treated, a young lady who was qualified to give laws to all her family!

When my cousins were told that the lid was unscrewed, they pressed in again, all but the mournful father and mother, as if by consent. Mrs. Hervey kissed her pale lips. Flower of the world! was all she could say; and gave place to Miss Arabella; who, kissing the forehead of *her* whom she had so cruelly treated, could only say to my Cousin James (looking upon the corpse, and upon him): O brother! While he, taking the fair lifeless hand, kissed it, and retreated with precipitation.

Her two uncles were speechless. They seemed to wait each other's example, whether to look upon the corpse or not. I ordered the lid to be replaced; and then they pressed forward, as the others again did, to take a last farewell of the casket which so lately contained so rich a jewel.

Then it was that the grief of each found fluent expression; and the fair corpse was addressed to, with all the tenderness that the sincerest love and warmest admiration could inspire; each according to their different degrees of relationship, as if none of them had before looked upon her. She was their *very* niece! both uncles said. The injured saint! her Uncle Harlowe. The same smiling sister! Arabella. The dear creature! all of them. The same benignity of countenance! The same sweet composure! The same natural dignity! *She* was questionless happy! That sweet smile betokened *her* being so; *themselves* most unhappy! And then, once more, the brother took the lifeless hand, and vowed revenge upon it, on the cursed author (ie. Lovelace) of all this distress.

The unhappy parents proposed to take one last view and farewell of their once darling daughter. The father was got to the parlour door, after the inconsolable mother: but neither of them was able to enter it. The mother said she must once more see the child of her heart, or she should never enjoy herself. But they both agreed to defer their melancholy curiosity till the next day; and hand in hand retired inconsolable, and speechless both, their faces overspread with woe, and turned from each other, as unable each to behold the distress of the other.

Clarissa, IV, cxl

And this is by no means the end of what the Colonel calls his 'doleful prolixity'; there are many more friends and relations yet to crowd about the corpse before it is fully interred. There is little doubt that Richardson shares the 'melancholy curiosity' of the Harlowes and cannot resist spying on his heroine until the last possible moment.

97

But this morbidity—and there was something of a cult of morbidity at the time—also derives from Richardson's strongly developed sense of physical things. His world is a solidly realistic one where objects take on their own special significance and value, and Clarissa's smiling corpse —no less than Pamela's bundles—still has a part to play in the action, if only as a harsh reminder to the Harlowes of their sterile materialism in regarding their daughter simply as a marriageable article. In other words the body still has an active role in the drama of remorse centred upon Harlowe Place. Notice also, how Richardson is intent upon the methodical arrangement of the scene (as before) in order to produce the greatest pathetic effect: Clarissa laid out at the centre of the stage; the almost processional rhythm of the relations as they come up in their turn; and the chorus-like chant of their grief—'their *very* niece!', 'The injured saint!', 'The dear creature!', the same this and the same that, and so on, all of which increases the sense of tragic inevitability. The tragedy being that just when the Harlowes are prepared to receive Clarissa back into the fold, they finally get the news of her death.

This kind of description, of course, can all too easily become too contrived and our suspicions are aroused when we are told that Colonel Morden would like Belford to comment upon his scene-painting. Belford, predictably, compliments the Colonel on his 'affecting descriptions' (IV, cxliv) and, once again, Richardson has complimented himself upon the usefulness of his writings. We must note, however, the contemporary acclamation that Richardson received for his achievement in the pathetic. Indeed, some of his readers found him almost too painful to read in some parts, and he was forced to advise Lady Bradshaigh for one, to 'Burn the Book when you come to the Scenes you cannot go thro' (*Letters* p. 97). He was speaking of *Clarissa*, but his readers found powerfully affecting scenes in the other two novels also, and certainly part of his great reputation and influence can be attributed to his success in this field.

The modern reader, however, is much more likely to read parody into some of Richardson's pathos, especially where it is too drawn out; and exclamatory phrases like 'Flower of the world!', and 'O brother!' will hardly prompt today the tearful reaction they undoubtedly did in the Richardsonian circle. Instead, we are much more likely to value a very different strain in Richardson's descriptive pieces, where sharp observation is put to humorous use. In fact the comic and the serious are very closely allied in Richardson's imagination. As we have seen, particularly in the description of Mrs. Jewkes, he can very easily turn an ugly shape into a grotesque one; a deadly strength into a waddling one. Something of the same knack can be seen in the following scene, where stronger emotions are furiously held in check, and a potentially serious occasion is transformed by the writer into an oddly ridiculous one. Clarissa has been begging her mother to soften her father's displeasure against her, and her mother has angrily replied.

36

She had hardly spoken the words when Shorey came in to tell her that Mr. Solmes was in the hall, and desired admittance.

Ugly creature! What, at the close of day, brought him hither? But, on second thoughts, I believe it was contrived, that he should be here at supper, to know the result of the conference between my mother and me, and that my father, on his return, might find us together.

I was hurrying away; but my mother commanded me (since I had come down only, as she said, to mock her) not to stir; and at the same time see if I could behave so to Mr. Solmes, as might encourage her to make the favourable report to my father which I had besought her to make.

My sister triumphed. I was vexed to be so caught, and to have such an angry and cutting rebuke given me, with an aspect more like the taunting sister than the indulgent mother, if I may presume to say so: for she herself seemed to enjoy the surprise upon me.

The man stalked in. His usual walk is by pauses, as if (from the same vacuity of thought which made Dryden's clown whistle) he was telling his steps: and first paid his clumsy respects to my mother; then to my sister; next to me, as if I were already his wife, and therefore to be last in his notice; and sitting down by me, told us in general what weather it was. Very cold he made it; but I was warm enough. Then addressing himself to me; and how do *you* find it, miss? was his question; and would have taken my hand.

I withdrew it, I believe with disdain enough. My mother frowned. My sister bit her lip.

I could not contain myself: I never was so bold in my life; for I went on with my plea as if Mr. Solmes had not been there.

My mother coloured, and looked at him, at my sister, and at me. My sister's eyes were opener and bigger than ever I saw them before.

The man understood me. He hemmed, and removed from one chair to another.

I went on, supplicating for my mother's favourable report: Nothing but invincible dislike, said I—

What would the girl be at, interrupted my mother?

Why, Clary! Is this a subject! Is this!—is this!—is this a time—and again she looked upon Mr. Solmes.

I am sorry, on reflection, that I put my mamma into so much confusion. To be sure it was very saucy in me.

I beg pardon, madam, said I. But my papa will soon return. And since I am not permitted to withdraw, it is not necessary, I humbly presume, that Mr. Solmes's presence should deprive me of this opportunity to implore your favourable report; and at the same time, if he still visit on my account (looking at him) to convince him, that it cannot possibly be to any purpose.

Is the girl mad? said my mother, interrupting me.

My sister, with the affectation of a whisper to my mother: This is—this is *spite*, madam (very *spitefully* she spoke the word) because you commanded her to stay.

I only looked at her, turning to my mother, Permit me, madam, said I, to repeat my request. I have no brother, no sister! If I lose my mamma's favour I am lost for ever!

Mr. Solmes removed to his first seat, and fell to gnawing the head of his hazel; a carved head, almost as ugly as his own—I did not think the man was so *sensible*.

My sister rose, with a face all over scarlet, and stepping to the table, where lay a fan, she took it up, and although Mr. Solmes had observed that the weather was cold, fanned herself very violently.

Clarissa, I, xxi

Although we begin ominously here, sharing Clarissa's feeling of repulsion at the very mention of Solmes—notice, for example, the association between Solmes, ugliness, and darkness—we are soon in the middle of a social comedy with Solmes as the clownish centrepiece. Comedy is achieved through surprise: instead of a maidenish shrinking away, Clarissa offers a saucy resistance, and from telling them what weather it was and generally commanding attention as an important visitor, Solmes is reduced to an embarrassed chair-shifting silence. Solmes, of course, is an insensitive brute, but here in the drawing-room arena, the advantage is all with Clarissa and we can enjoy not only the actual flouting of the predatory suitor, but also the spiteful asides that Clarissa brings into her account. In this enjoyment, we are temporarily distracted—and Clarissa too perhaps—from the real difficulties which still confront her.

A sharpness of observation bordering often on spiteful-ness is indeed a characteristic talent of the Richardsonian female. It is also, of course, one of the strongest weapons in Richardson's own armoury, and few novelists have dealt so successfully with the mannerisms and gestures of the social scene. In *Grandison*, we can see his talent for this kind of writing at its best, and for the skilful rendering of a situation in all its humorous aspects one can hardly do better than to turn to this novel. We shall conclude, there-fore, with an extract which illustrates the situational comedy in the opening letters of *Grandison*, the germ of which, we have seen in the courting situation above. Harriet Byron is writing to her friend about the fashionable company she met at Lady Betty Williams's London house, the foppish Sir Hargrave being the most interesting.

37

But mutual civilities had hardly passed, when Lady Betty, having been called out, returned, introducing, as a gentle-man who would be acceptable to every one, Sir Hargrave Pollexfen. He is, whispered she to me, as he saluted the rest of the company in a very gallant manner, a young baronet of a very large estate, the greatest part of which has lately come to him by the death of a grandmother, and two uncles, all very rich.

When he was presented to me, by name, and I to him; I think myself very happy, said he, in being admitted to the presence of a young lady so celebrated for her graces of person and mind. Then, addressing himself to Lady Betty, Much did I hear, when I was at the last Northampton races, of Miss Byron: but little did I expect to find report fall so short of what I see.

Miss Cantillon bridled, played with her fan, and looked as if she thought herself slighted; a little scorn intermingled with the airs she gave herself.

Miss Clements smiled, and looked pleased, as if she enjoyed, good-naturedly, a compliment made to one of the sex which she adorns by the goodness of her heart.

Miss Barnvelt said, she had from the moment I first entered, beheld me with the eye of a lover. And freely taking my hand, squeezed it.—Charming creature! said she, as if addressing a country innocent, and perhaps expecting me to be covered with blushes and confusion.

The baronet excusing himself to Lady Betty, assured her, that she must place this his bold intrusion to the account of Miss Byron, he having been told that she was to be there.

Whatever were his motive, Lady Betty said, he did her favour; and she was sure the whole company would think themselves *doubly* obliged to Miss Byron.

The student looked as if he thought himself eclipsed by Sir Hargrave, and as if, in revenge, he was putting his fine speeches into Latin, and trying them by the rules of grammar, a broken sentence from a classic author bursting from his lips; and, at last standing up, half on tip-toe (as if he wanted to look down upon the baronet) he stuck one hand in his side, and passed by him, casting a contemptuous eye on his gaudy dress.

Mr. Singleton smiled, and looked as if delighted with all

he saw and heard. Once, indeed, he tried to speak: his mouth actually opened to give passage to his words, as sometimes seems to be his way before the words are quite ready: but he sat down satisfied with the effort.

It is true, people who do not make themselves contemptible by affectation should not be despised. Poor and rich, wise and unwise, we are all links of the same great chain. And you must tell me, my dear, if I, in endeavouring to give true descriptions of the persons I see, incur the censure I pass on others who despise any one for defects they cannot help.

Sir Charles Grandison, I, x

Each figure is caught exactly at the right vulnerable moment for exposure in a series of camera-like stills. As always in Richardson, the all-important detail is unfailingly taken in (remember Solmes's attack on the head of his stick): Miss Cantillon's 'bridling', the jerky individual movements of the student, and Singleton's satisfaction at the mere opening of his mouth. Each detail unerringly pinpoints the character for us. Harriet's sharp intelligence (like that of a Jane Austen heroine—Richardson's influence on Jane Austen has often been noted) plays over the whole scene, and each idiosyncracy is caught by her cataloguing eye. This impressive account only breaks down with the intrusive piety of the last paragraph—the goody-goody reflections that we are all 'links of the same great chain'. Having been convinced by Richardson's superb puppetry of the foolishness of the social animal, it is too much to expect us to reverence it almost in the same breath.

Richardson's social observation, then, is remarkably incisive, and the main strength of his writing comes from his ability to give new life to daily trivia. We shall close, therefore, with a humorous self-portrait which, perhaps best of all, sums up these gifts. As he walks through the park, he tells Lady Bradshaigh, his eye is always

. . . on the ladies; if they have very large hoops, he looks down and supercilious, and as if he would be thought wise, but perhaps the sillier for that: as he approaches a lady, his eye is never fixed first upon her face, but upon her feet, and thence he raises it up, pretty quickly for a dull eye; and one would think (if we thought him at all worthy of observation) that from her air and (the last beheld) her face, he sets her down in his mind as *so* or *so*, and then passes on to the next object he meets; only then looking back, if he greatly likes or dislikes, as if he would see if the lady appear to be all of a piece, in the one light or in the other.

Letters, p. 136

Here we have it all: the feminine interest, the sharp observation, the humorous slyness; these are the qualities which made a great novelist out of the sober man of business.

A note on Richardson and Fielding

Quite inevitably, Richardson's name has always been coupled with Fielding's. Fielding's first excursions into prose fiction—*Shamela* and *Joseph Andrews*—were both prompted by the moral ambivalences in *Pamela*. Richardson's attitude towards Fielding thereafter was always very bitter, though Fielding paid generous tribute to his other work. The personal antipathy between the two, however, can easily obscure the more important differences between their approaches to the novel as a fictional form.

Fielding's approach was much more scholarly than Richardson's, and he writes with a full awareness of the classical literary tradition. His formula for his own kind of fiction—'the comic epic in prose'—is clearly derived from his knowledge of the great epic writers of the past, and his breadth of learning allows him to employ rhetoric and mock-heroic towards satirical ends. Richardson, on the other hand, had no formal scholarship and writes from his own experience of contemporary life. As a moralist in fact he is frankly suspicious of the classical tradition and

tends to equate learning with sophistry, favouring directness much more than irony.

As one might expect from this, Fielding is much more
self-conscious about his art than Richardson, and far from
limiting himself to straightforward narration, discusses all
manner of critical ideas as he goes along. His sense of
detachment is very quickly passed on to the reader, and the
novel itself is never in danger of being mistaken for real
life. Fielding's intrusions at the expense of the 'life flow'
of the novel might be likened to those of a demonstrator
at a showing of picture slides: the flow of pictures is
frequently arrested while some point is explained, or an
observation made. Richardson, in contrast, is anxious that
nothing should interrupt the lifelike flow of action and
thought; he is after the reader's involvement not his detachment. The effect here is more like that of the uninter-
rupted film, where the spectator can lose his sense of the
normal everyday context which might distract his involvement.

Fielding's awareness of the historical context, and
Richardson's rather obvious lack of it, also affects their
approach towards characterisation. Fielding keeps his eye
upon mankind in general rather than upon individuals,
and produces a series of general types. Our knowledge of
these characters is, of course, entirely external, and it is
important that it should be so for Fielding's comic purpose.
If we are to laugh at the follies of mankind, and perhaps
at our own, we must keep these characters in mind as
examples, and not become too involved with their lives.
Richardson, as we know, works very differently, projecting
himself into his characters, and making us feel that they
develop in response to experience.

Fielding's plots also differ markedly from Richardson's.

His concern to comment at large upon human nature leads him to adopt the picaresque type of narrative, where the hero in wandering along the highroad enables the author to make extensive observations about society. One adventure follows another with seeming randomness, but the impression is adequately given of a thorough encounter with all kinds of life. Such a method also allows the author a rich opportunity for boisterous humour and farce. Richardson, on the other hand, has no use for the picaresque narrative; he is concerned with the close situation, with emotional pressures where restrictedness in fact becomes a function of the plot. To put it very crudely, most of Fielding's actions take place as energetic realities, while most of Richardson's take place in the minds of his characters.

Other differences between the two novelists are determined largely by the different character of their moral outlook. Both are serious moralists, but each emphasised different aspects of morality and used different methods of inculcating it. Fielding tries to laugh mankind out of its viciousness, Richardson tries to shock it back to paths of virtue. Fielding, as a former dramatist, sees the comedy of manners and highlights absurdity by holding it at a distance. He successfully sets the particular experience into a universal context, and provides a continuous perspective for judgment. Richardson takes us in another direction, into the private world of the individual consciousness; a world essentially in isolation from Fielding's context. Dr. Johnson is said to have remarked that 'Richardson had picked the kernel of life . . . while Fielding was contented with the husk': although the remark is disparaging to Fielding, it does usefully distinguish their separate areas of investigation.

Bibliography

Original editions

Letters Written to and for Particular Friends on the most Important Occasions, 1741.
Pamela: Or Virtue Rewarded, 4 vols., Part I, 1740, Part II, 1741.
Clarissa: Or the History of a Young Lady, 7 vols., 1748.
The History of Sir Charles Grandison, 7 vols., 1754.
A Collection of the Moral and Instructive Sentiments . . . Contained in the Histories of Pamela, Clarissa, and Sir Charles Grandison, 1755.

Modern editions

Familiar Letters on Important Occasions, with an introduction by B. W. Downs, G. Routledge, London, 1928.
Pamela, with an introduction by M. Kinkead-Weekes, 2 vols., Everyman's Library, 1962.
Pamela, with an introduction by W. M. Sale (Part I only), The Norton Library, New York, 1958.

Clarissa, with an introduction by J. Butt, 4 vols., Every-man's Library, 1962.

Grandison is not available separately, but may be found in these collected editions.

The Works, with a Prefatory Chapter of Biographical Criticism by L. Stephen, 12 vols., London, 1883.

The Novels, with a Life of the Author and Introduction by W. L. Phelps, 19 vols., New York, 1902.

The Novels, with an introduction by E. M. M. McKenna, 20 vols., London, 1902.

The Novels, 18 vols., Shakespeare Head Edition, Oxford, 1929–31.

Of the various abridgements of *Grandison*, by far the best is:

Letters From Sir Charles Grandison, Selected with a Biographical Introduction and Connecting Notes by George Saintsbury, 2 vols., London, 1895.

Select critical bibliography

For convenience, the following have been divided chronologically into:

(*a*) General introductory material, (*b*) Major biographical and critical studies, and (*c*) Short articles dealing with special topics.

(*a*) All the standard Histories of English Literature deal at length with Richardson, but the following are probably the most useful to begin with:

KETTLE, A., *An Introduction to the English Novel*, vol. I, Hutchinson University Lib., London and New York, 1951, Grey Arrow ed., 1962.

ALLEN, W., *The English Novel*, Phoenix House, London, 1954, Penguin Books, London and Baltimore, 1958.

FORD, BORIS (ed.), *The Pelican Guide to English Literature*, vol. IV, Penguin Books, 1957. Has a good chapter on Richardson by F. Bradbrook.

BRISSENDEN, R. F., *Samuel Richardson*, Writers and their Work No. 101, Longmans, Green & Co., London and New York, 1958. A very lucid and concise introduction.

(b)

DOWNS, B. W., *Richardson*, G. Routledge, London, 1928. Contains some of the finest criticism to date, and also sets Richardson firmly in his times.

KRUTCH, J. W., *Five Masters*, Jonathan Cape, London and New York, 1931. Tends to capitalise on Richardson's foibles, but well worth reading.

SINGER, G. F., *The Epistolary Novel*, University of Pennsylvania Press, Philadelphia, 1933. An informed account of Richardson, along with a history of the whole genre of epistolary writing.

MCKILLOP, A. D., *Samuel Richardson, Printer & Novelist*, University of North Carolina Press, Chapel Hill, 1936. A key reference work by a noted scholar of Richardson's work.

PRITCHETT, V. S., *The Living Novel*, Chatto & Windus, London, 1946. Contains a chapter on *Clarissa* with some lively and provocative criticism.

HILLES, F. W. (ed.), *The Age of Johnson*, Yale University Press, New Haven, 1949, Yale Paperbound ed., 1964. Includes an excellent essay on Richardson's social and moral attitudes, by W. M. Sale, Jr.

GHENT, D. VAN, *The English Novel, Form & Function*, Rinehart & Co., New York, 1953, Harper Torchbook ed., 1961. Contains a brilliant though difficult essay on *Clarissa*.

MCKILLOP, A. D., *The Early Masters of English Fiction*, Univ. of Kansas Press, Lawrence, 1956. Richardson placed alongside his contemporaries. A very thorough and intelligent account.

DAICHES, D., *Literary Essays*, Oliver & Boyd, London, 1956. Contains some perceptive remarks on Richardson.

WATT, I., *The Rise of the Novel*, Chatto & Windus, London, 1957, Peregrine ed. (Penguin Books), 1963. Indispensable for a real understanding of the social and literary background, with some first-rate chapters on *Pamela* and *Clarissa*.

KREISSMAN, B., *Pamela-Shamela*, University of Nebraska Studies No. 22, Lincoln, 1960. An entertaining account of the parodic literature which followed the appearance of *Pamela*.

GOLDEN, M., *Richardson's Characters*, University of Michigan Press, Ann Arbor, 1963. A psychological study of the characters in the light of Richardson's own fantasies. Somewhat over-emphatic, but highly intriguing.

(c)

KERMODE, F., 'Richardson and Fielding', *The Cambridge Journal*, IV, 1950, now reprinted in *Essays on the Eighteenth Century Novel*, ed. R. D. Spector, University of Indiana Press, Bloomington, 1965. A very useful discussion of their respective literary reputations.

MCKILLOP, A. D., *Epistolary Technique in Richardson*, The Rice Institute Pamphlet, XXXVIII, April 1951. A detailed study of Richardson's narrative control.

HILL, C., 'Clarissa Harlowe and Her Times', *Essays in Criti-*

cism, V, October 1955. Relates the novel to its historical context, and makes interesting suggestions about Richardson's real purpose.

WATT, I., 'Samuel Richardson', *The Listener*, February 4th, 1965. Considers Richardson as an 'innovator', and deals excellently with *Pamela*.

KEARNEY, A. M., 'Clarissa and the Epistolary Form', *Essays in Criticism*, XVI, January 1966. Deals with Richardson's narrative method in relation to his tragic purpose.

The above are representative of modern criticism, but some valuable insights are contained in earlier studies, particularly in the introductions to the collected editions of the novels. Of these, Leslie Stephen's to the 1883 edition deserves a special mention.